Simon Brett

Another Little Sod!

How to Be a Little Sod. Book 3

illustrated by
Tony Ross

ORION

To ELIZABETH MOTLEY
(who will understand)

An Orion Paperback
First published in Great Britain in 1997
by Victor Gollancz
This paperback edition published in 1999 by
Orion Books Ltd,
Orion House, 5 Upper St Martin's Lane,
London WC2H 9EA

A CIP catalogue record for this book
is available from the British Library.

ISBN: 0 75282 730 8

Printed and bound in Great Britain by
Clays Ltd, St Ives plc

Twenty-Fifth Month

DAY 1

I face my third year with great confidence. I'm much bigger and more mature. I have remarkable manual dexterity. I can eat with a spoon when I feel like it – but fingers are more fun. I can manage an ordinary cup as opposed to a sucky cup – again when I feel like it, which is most of the time, because ordinary cups make more mess. I can even sometimes keep dry in Trainer Pants – but I rarely feel like that.

And I have a vocabulary of nearly two hundred words – though the actual language some of them belong to has yet to be invented.

In fact, I'm a pretty smooth operator with a great many highly developed skills. And how am I going to use those skills during my third year?

You've guessed it. I will use them for the same noble purpose to which I dedicated my first two years – making my parents' life hell!

Give them their due, though, they do sometimes make an effort. Today, for instance, they arranged a birthday party for me. Both took the afternoon off work, which is quite something. They'd really pushed the boat out – lots of cakes, jellies, crisps, etc. And a great pile of sweetie-bags for me.

Great, I thought. Finally my parents are giving me the lifestyle I deserve.

Then they went and spoiled it all by inviting a whole bunch of other toddlers to share the goodies! They even invited the most despised object in the world – Baby Einstein, who was born round the same time as me and has since then driven me mad by making every developmental advance months before I've even thought about it.

At least I saw to it today that Baby Einstein went home wiping cream and jelly out of tear-stained eyes.

But the worst thing was – my parents gave the sweetie-bags away to all the other toddlers! I was only left with one! Talk about mean.

Next time I have a birthday party, I'll choose the guest list. And there won't be anyone else on it.

On the other hand, I do get more presents this way. All the guest toddlers brought me something.

By the way, at the end of last year, my parents came up with what I can only assume was their idea of a joke: they pretended they were going to have another baby. I'm glad to say I haven't heard any more of that nonsense since. There is no New Baby on the way.

A VOICE FROM THE WOMB:

Don't you believe it, sunshine.

I exist all right. Oh yes, indeedy.

It's pretty funny and dark in here. Kind of squelchy, too . . . But listen, don't anyone try to ignore me, because I'm very much here.

OK, maybe I am only 2.2 centimetres long. Maybe I do still bear more resemblance to a tadpole than a baby, but I very definitely exist, and I'm keeping a beady eye on what's going on out there.

I am developing at an incredible speed. Only a couple of days ago – I got nostrils! Wow! What a blast! I can't stuff things up them yet, but I will be able to one day. So that's something to look forward to.

Just remember – I'm an embryo with attitude. This is a womb with a view.

DAY 2

They've got a nerve! I would have thought my behaviour yesterday had made my views on the subject absolutely clear, and yet this afternoon I'm packed off to Baby Einstein's birthday party! (Not only always more advanced than me, the little creep is also a day younger.)

Still, the same ammunition was to hand, so I saw to it that Baby Einstein ended a second party wiping cream and jelly out of tear-stained eyes.

My dad left work early to pick me up. I was given a sweetie-bag as I was leaving and He said jokingly to my hostess, 'Maybe I should take another one for the New Baby when it arrives . . . ?'

If they want to keep going on about the New Baby, I suppose that's up to them. I don't care. I got two sweetie-bags out of it.

DAY 4

Saturday. Had a bit of an argument with my mum today. It was on a matter of logic, which has never been Her strong point.

It was to do with my wellies. She wanted me to put my socks on before I put my wellies on. I, on the other hand, wanted to put my wellies on first, and then see if She could get my socks on over them.

We argued about this for an hour or so. I was quite happy to – I enjoy the cut-and-thrust of debate – but She didn't seem to be enjoying it quite as much. She kept bringing up arguments about the fact that my socks would get wet, or that my feet would get chafed in the wellies. But as always She kept missing the really important point – that what I was suggesting would be a lot more FUN.

Eventually, in a tone of something approaching exasperation, She said, 'I know what the trouble with you is. You're just going through "The Terrible Twos".'

This was not an expression I'd heard before. Still, if She thinks I'm going through 'The Terrible Twos', I'll make absolutely certain I live up to it. After all, I wouldn't want to disappoint Her.

DAY 10

My days have settled into a kind of routine. She still goes out to work. I have endlessly tried to make Her understand that She shouldn't be doing this, that She's failing in Her duties towards me, and that She'd be much more fulfilled doing what She should be doing – staying home, pandering to my every whim, and reacting with amazed delight to my every new developmental advance. But will She listen? No.

As a result, daytimes during the week I am looked after by this Mother's Help who I call the Juggernaut. She is a young woman blessed with neither beauty nor high intelligence. In fact, she'd be very sad sack indeed, except that she has something that makes her the envy of the known world. She has the high honour of looking after me.

DAY 12

I've now got my own private flotation tank – very swish. Yes, I've got all this amniotic fluid around me, and I can just swoosh to and fro . . . to and fro . . .

Very luxurious.

To and fro . . . to and fro . . .

Mind you, it's not very interesting. I may have a strong point of view, but I haven't got much of an actual view. I mean, my eyes are fully formed now, but it's a bit difficult to say for sure whether they work or not when you're just swooshing around in the darkness.

Still, maybe I can liven things up by trying some more elaborate movements. My very own synchronized swimming routine, that'd be good. Maybe some kind of complicated backflip or—

Hey! I've just noticed something. I thought I was free-floating down here, but I'm not. I'm actually moored to the side by this kind of rope thing. Hmm, that's going to cramp my style a bit when it comes to the old amniotic aerobics.

Oh well, never mind . . . Not much I can do about it.

Here we go again. To and fro . . . to and fro . . .

DAY 16

To and fro . . . to and fro . . .
  This is really boring.
  To and fro . . . to and fro . . .

Maybe if I kicked on the side, somebody would hear me and come and let me out . . . ?

One – two – three. Big kick!

Nothing. Not a sausage. I don't think anyone heard that, or felt it. I'm too little, you see. I have grown, but I'm still only 6.5 centimetres long. That's not very big, is it? I mean, if a fisherman caught me, he'd definitely throw me back.

To and fro . . . to and fro . . .

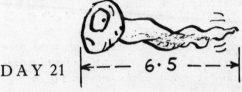

DAY 21

Another toddler came round to play with me today. If that makes it sound like a big social event, don't get me wrong. It's simply a system the Juggernaut and the other Mother's Help have worked out, so that each of them alternately gets a chance to go off shopping on her own.

I loathe the other toddler, and the feeling seems to be mutual. I call it the Crybaby, because I can always make it cry.

Call me old-fashioned, but I don't think you can beat the well-placed finger in the eye. Never fails to get the Crybaby going.

DAY 24

There's a basic rule with parents: they love making rods for their own backs. Self-beating rods have the same fascination for parents as a sheer cliff-face has for the average lemming.

Take food, for example. I am now an extremely faddy eater. And it's entirely Her fault. Another perfect example of the Rod For Her Own Back Syndrome.

It's down to the range of food that I'm given. Once they're firmly on to solid foods, babies will eat virtually anything that doesn't actually cause corrosion in their tiny mouths.

And yet the stuff we eat – at least in this country – is as bland as if it'd been processed by a New Labour spin-doctor. The bulk of my diet for the last year has come out of those little tins and packets that have names like comedy double acts – Lamb and Peas, Chicken and Tomato, Liver and Spinach, etc. And, as I have observed in an earlier *oeuvre**, they all taste absolutely identical – just like soggy cardboard.

The trouble is, a diet of soggy cardboard blunts the old taste-buds. They get slack and lazy, and they can't cope with the shock of suddenly eating something that's got some FLAVOUR.

So, when this evening She, obedient to the instructions in one of Her childcare books, tried to introduce my enfeebled taste-buds to something a bit more exotic, it got a very firm thumbs-down.

I'm not sure what it was. Something they'd been eating, something mildly spicy, something that I'll probably develop a passionate taste for when I'm a student and living away from home for the first time.

But there was no way my infant taste-buds, softened by a continuing diet of soggy cardboard, could cope with the alien sensation of FOOD THAT ACTU-ALLY TASTED OF SOMETHING.

---

* *How to Be a Little Sod* – What do you mean you haven't read it?

I expressed my displeasure in my usual manner, by hurling the dish from my high chair. Blessed by the kind of luck that only comes when you're on a roll, I saw the dish land, neatly upturned, on the cat's head.

Sorry, Mum. I'm afraid your hopes of doing what the childcare book says, and 'slowly introducing new tastes into the baby's diet until he or she is eating just the same as the rest of the family', are doomed to failure. No, you're going to have to cook me separate meals for many years to come. Oh, the power!

DAY 25

Decided what my future diet will be. Junk food from the freezer: fish fingers, beefburgers, oven chips, all that stuff. And never anything that has a hint of green about it. Nothing that vaguely resembles a fresh vegetable. YUK, no way.

It's not that I particularly like one sort of food more than another. But this is a power struggle, and I need to make the terms of engagement absolutely clear.

Also, I need some kind of comeback for all the sanctimonious sentences I've heard Her say to Her right-on friends beginning, 'No child of mine will ever be allowed to . . .'

'No child of mine will ever be allowed to eat oven chips.'

'No child of mine will ever be allowed to eat sweets between meals.'

Oh, I love giving Her Her comeuppance. Having a baby who's addicted to junk food is going to lose Her loads of street cred.

I don't know what She's complaining about, though. Except for one brief phase of only eating crisps and satsumas, I've been very restrained on the food-fad front. My mum doesn't know how lucky She is.

DAY 26

Hmm, pity I can't yet make Her look silly on the old 'No child of mine will ever be allowed to smoke' front, but they don't have any cigarettes round the house and, anyway, I'm not sure that my tiny fingers could cope with a lighter.

But don't worry, the day will come.

DAY 29

To and fro . . . to and fro . . .
I'm really seriously bored now.
Maybe I should try something different . . . ?
Fro and to . . . fro and to . . .

DAY 31

The Juggernaut did something unforgivable today. She threw away Gooey!

Gooey, perhaps I should explain, is a cuddly frog. No, actually, that's inaccurate. Gooey *was* a cuddly frog.

One of Her friends gave him to me . . . I think it was the Christmas before last. At the time I took no notice of it at all. It was my first Christmas and I was pretending to be more interested in the wrapping paper than the presents – well, it kept them amused.

But some months later my mum, in desperation to find something to distract my attention for more than thirty seconds, dug deep into the toy cupboard and produced Gooey.

Well, I did a bit more token screaming to show I wasn't to be won over too easily, but I did rather fancy playing with a cuddly frog.

Over the next few months I pretended to get quite attached to Gooey. I'd carry him around with me a lot of the time, and I'd make a fuss if they tried to put me to bed without him. I didn't really care about him – it's hard to build up much of an emotional relationship with a stuffed lump of cloth – but recognizing that Gooey could provide many useful ways of infuriating my parents, I continued the pretence.

In fact, Gooey really took over from my imaginary friend, Dirpy. Imaginary friends are all very well in their way, but they do involve you in a lot of talking. Saying 'You can't sit in that chair. It's Dirpy's chair' is quite hard work, but with Gooey I've never had to say anything. If Gooey was sitting in a chair, it was perfectly obvious it must be Gooey's chair. So I saved my breath and just bawled my head off if anyone sat on Gooey or tried to move him.

But, though nobody else was allowed to touch him, *I* subjected Gooey to every possible indignity I could. Everywhere I went, I dragged him round on a piece of string. I spent a lot of time sucking and chewing him.

I Peed over him, I Pooed over him, I threw up over him. I rubbed food, sand and mud into him. I chucked him down the loo. (He got stuck and they had to get the plumber in. That pleased them no end.) I threw him out of my buggy into any puddles we happened to pass. And whenever the opportunity arose, I chucked him into the cat's food bowl.

Now cuddly frogs are not, on the whole, built for

durability, and my treatment of Gooey pretty quickly reduced him to a terrible state. This was made worse by the fact that he spent such a large proportion of his life in the washing machine and the rest of the time in my mouth. My mum was in a constant state of nervous anxiety about GERMS.

'Oh, no!' She'd shriek. 'Don't put that in your mouth! You don't know where it's been!'

This was absolute nonsense. I knew exactly where it had been. After all, I was the one who'd put it there.

Well, going through the full wash-cycle of a washing machine at least once a day for eight months doesn't do the average cuddly frog a lot of good.

Gradually Gooey started to lose his stuffing, and as I chewed and sucked at him over the months, he slowly deflated like a punctured Lilo. Now, when he's laid flat on the floor, he looks like a bit of motorway road-kill.

But has this physical deterioration stopped my shows of apparent affection for the grubby little rag? No, I have become more devoted to Gooey than ever.

So today, when I went shopping with the Juggernaut, I ensured that Gooey was clutched to my chest throughout the expedition.

It was on the way back that the crisis occurred. I was out of my buggy and walking the last bit home (something I do these days, when I feel like it). And on the pavement, just near our house, was this huge pile of fresh Dog Poo.

Well, I did the obvious thing.

I dropped Gooey right in it, and put my foot on top to grind him in.

The result was that not only Gooey but also my shoe was covered with the stuff.

Then, as the Juggernaut rushed forward to pull me away, I lost my balance and toppled sideways, so that I ended up sitting in it too. There was Dog Poo all over my dungarees.

It was after she'd got me all cleaned and changed that the Juggernaut did the unforgivable thing.

Picking up Gooey with a pair of wooden tongs, she said, 'We'll never get the GERMS off this. Say good-bye to Gooey now. I'm afraid I'm going to put him straight into the dustbin.' And she did exactly that.

What made it worse was that today's the day the dustbin men come.

I bawled for the rest of the afternoon.

I didn't actually care that much, but I've always recognized a good thing to make a fuss about when I've seen one.

When She came home from work, the Juggernaut told Her what had happened. Give Her Her due, my mum did say, 'Oh, I'm not sure you should have done that. Gooey's very important to Baby, you know.'

I wouldn't be comforted. I bawled all evening.

I bawled all night.

And the word that kept recurring in the midst of my pitiful wails was, 'Gooey! Gooey! Gooey!'

It would have been enough to break a heart of stone.

Twenty-Sixth Month

DAY 3

I saw to it that they got no sleep last night.

And I saw to it that the Juggernaut got no peace during the day. She had to be made to realize the enormity of her crime in having thrown Gooey away.

I can modestly state that I was entirely successful in my efforts. The Juggernaut is not a woman renowned for her sensitivity, but today I made her feel as though she was a creature somewhere on the evolutionary scale below worms, slugs, replacement window salesmen and politicians.

Then, when my mum came back from work, I made Her feel awful too.

Still, She had at least made an effort. She'd brought back a present for me. It was a brand-new cuddly frog, brightly coloured and absolutely identical to Gooey – before I started working on him.

My first thought was, Ooh, I think that's rather nice. It's much better than that smelly rag I've been lugging around for months. I almost reached out to take it, before good sense prevailed.

No, the new cuddly frog wasn't my Gooey! I hated it! How could they fob me off with just any old Gooey! She mustn't judge me by Her own standards. I wasn't fickle like Her. I wanted *my* Gooey!

So I spent the evening bawling my head off yet again.

And I continued late into the night, my sobs still punctuated with heart-rending cries of, 'Gooey! Gooey! Gooey!'

DAY 4

At about four this morning, as I bawled on, I heard them talking in their bedroom. Talking? It was more like arguing. She was trying to persuade Him to do something, and He was saying that He was too tired and didn't want to.

This was quite interesting. Usually, in such conversations, it's the other way round.

Eventually there was a commotion, angry sounds of Him getting out of bed and getting dressed. Then He stumped downstairs and out of the front door, slamming it behind Him, with a shout of, 'Bloody Gooey! I'm a grown man. Why should I have to go off chasing bloody frogs!'

Since it sounded as though something was at last being done about Gooey, I allowed myself to doze off blissfully . . .

. . . and didn't wake up till half-past ten . . .

. . . to find, to my surprise, that She was still at home. She'd rung work to say She wouldn't be in, and She'd given the Juggernaut the day off. 'I thought I'd wait till Daddy came back,' She said.

I was puzzled, but I wasn't going to complain. She was going to spend the day looking after me – exactly what She should have been doing all this time instead of making futile attempts to pick up Her career where She'd left off.

I made sure She was kept busy all day. She did look terribly tired, and was having difficulty bending down and crawling on the floor with all that weight She's carrying now.

It's Her own fault. She ought to go on a diet.

It was four o'clock in the afternoon when He finally came in. And it was an entrance worth waiting for.

He was absolutely filthy, festooned with scraps and shreds of rubbish, and smelling like a local authority rubbish tip.

And in His hand He held . . . Gooey.

Filthy, smelly, disgusting, still covered with Dog Poo, but undeniably the original Gooey.

'There, look,' She said. 'Your Daddy's been all the way to the local authority rubbish tip to find Gooey for you! What a nice, kind, thoughtful Daddy you've got!'

You'd never have known it from the expression on His face.

He went off, complaining, to have a bath, while Gooey was put straight into the washing machine. After he'd had a full wash cycle and an hour in the drier, both parents came into the sitting room where I was watching television, holding out the colourless frog shape towards me.

'There,' She said. 'We've got your Gooey back for you, haven't we? What do you say to that?'

What could I say? I ignored Gooey all evening.

DAY 5

Didn't mention Gooey once today.

DAY 6

Or today. Went to bed without him, and made no fuss at all.

DAY 7

No mention of Gooey today either. Overheard Her saying to Him, 'Do you know, I think that little business of Gooey being lost may have cured the dependency. Baby's growing up. Doesn't need a Comfort Blanket any more.'

Oh no?

DAY 8

Today we were going to visit Her parents. This usually causes a few problems between Him and Her. Her parents are sticklers for punctuality, and my dad tends to bé a bit more laid-back about things. She is always panicky that they're going to be late.

And they're both always panicky about how I'm going to behave. When I'm at my grandparents', I cease to be an ordinary baby and become a visual aid in some long-running argument between my mum and Her mum about different approaches to childcare. Their particular battleground at the moment is over the subject of Toilet Training.

Her mum, who belongs to the Gestapo School of Toilet Training, thinks I should have been out of nappies much sooner. My mum, who's now got me more or less reliable during the day in Trainer Pants, regards this achievement as a vindication of her more casual approach. But tension on the subject remains.

Still, in the run-up to today's departure, everything seemed fine. My parents got together everything they needed. (Well, actually most of it was stuff *I* needed. Moving all my equipment round the country makes the logistics of the Gulf War look easy-peasy.) They got me dressed in the many layers I require during the cold weather. They coped with my sudden demand to do a Poo just as we were about to depart. They didn't even lose their tempers when it turned out to be a false alarm and I just did a Pee.

And they still managed to leave in plenty of time to arrive on schedule at my grandparents.

I waited until we'd been driving about twenty minutes before I started. Then, suddenly ... 'Want Gooey!' I screamed. 'Want Gooey!'

'Well, you can't bloody have Gooey!' said my dad, the tension of the moment getting to His temper.

'Want Gooey! Want Gooey!'

They only lasted another five minutes. Just as I thought, my mum started calculating the percentages. Was it preferable to arrive on time and have me behaving like the worst kind of Little Sod all day because I hadn't got Gooey? Or was it better to cut their losses, pacify me by going back to get Gooey, and weather the sniffs of disapproval prompted by the fact that we'd arrived late?

They turned round to get Gooey.

I pretended to be very pleased to have him back, and was silent for the rest of the journey to my grandparents' house.

When we finally arrived, while Her mum was sniffing with disapproval, and my mum was apologizing, I thought I'd remind them who was calling the shots here.

So I did a huge great Poo in my Trainer Pants.

This got them going on the Toilet Training argument again: it smouldered on merrily all day.

And, just to enrich the atmosphere, I did behave like the worst kind of Little Sod.

DAY 9

Plenty of time to think in here. I often wonder who the old Camper Van carrying me around actually is . . .

I quite fancy being born into the Royal Family . . .

Certainly want my parents to be well-heeled. Being born to money gives you such an advantage over the rest of the riff-raff out there.

DAY 14

It snowed today. I've seen the stuff before, but last year I wasn't really developed enough to take full advantage of it. This year I think it could be real FUN!

The Crybaby came round again. I pushed it over and rubbed its face in the snow. And sure enough, it started crying.

You know, it's hard to think of a nickname that was ever more apt.

DAY 15

Since it was the weekend, they had no excuse for not taking me out in the snow. Well, I say 'they', but in fact He was the one who got lumbered. She's still doing this stupid routine about feeling sick in the mornings.

So pleading nausea, She said that He could jolly well take me out in the snow. I'd been given a little sledge for Christmas, and He could jolly well take me out on that. 'Snow's so magical for them when they're tiny,' She said winsomely.

His expression suggested 'magical' wasn't the word He'd have chosen to describe the snow. I don't think it's the one He'd have chosen to describe me either. With a face like thunder, He started to get me dressed for the Arctic conditions outside.

Now getting dressed has always been one of the major daily outlets for completely awful behaviour, but the potential is even greater when there's snow about. Because for snow you need so many layers of clothes.

And each layer is a new opportunity for Parental Aggravation. As He found out this morning.

Recently I've refined my technique for driving a parent mad while being dressed. Six months ago I would just scream and use various predictable physical techniques. These included:

1. Going into 'The Starfish Position' (described in greater detail in *How to Be a Little Sod**).
2. Ensuring that, whatever garment is being put on, arms go into neck-holes or leg-holes, and legs go into arm-holes or neck-holes. Heads go in wherever they're likely to cause most trouble.

3. Suddenly letting one's limbs go as limp as cooked spaghetti, so that they can't be pushed into any arm-holes, leg-holes, etc.
4. Pulling all limbs immediately out of any arm-holes, leg-holes, etc. they may inadvertently have got inserted into.

* What do you mean – you still haven't read it!

That always worked OK, but it was pretty unsophisticated stuff compared to what I do now. The difference is that now I can talk.

Let me remind those of you who've forgotten the words of wisdom from my previous book (and I hope you feel suitably ashamed if you have) that the most valuable phrases for use in encounters with parents are the following: 'Me help!' or 'Me do it!'

These simple words can totally destroy them. They have spent over two years of their lives trying to get you to do things on your own. 'Come on, you can put on your own jumper, can't you?' 'Come on, you can lift that up for yourself, can't you?' 'Come on, you can help Mummy/Daddy do this, can't you?'

So, when you finally give them what they've been asking for, you don't have to modify your behaviour one little bit. You can be as obstreperous, bloody-minded and infuriating as before. But now, whatever you do, you fix an earnest expression on your face and keep on saying, 'Me help!' and 'Me do it!'

For a long time your parents will have no alternative but to believe you're genuinely trying to be helpful. They've read all the childcare books, so they know that your motor skills take a while to become fully developed; they know that you must be allowed time for trial and error; they know they must be patient while you work out how to do things for yourself.

And it drives them bloody mad! Tee-hee!

This morning was probably my finest demonstration to date of these new techniques, and my efforts reduced Him to a gibbering, incoherent wreck (even more so than usual, that is).

Let me start by listing the garments he had to get me into before I could be taken out into the snow. There were Trainer Pants and vest, T-shirt, two jumpers, woolly tights, dungarees, all-in-one waterproof zip-up number, woolly hat, gloves, two pairs of socks . . . and wellies.

Me do it
Me help

I made sure that not a single item of clothing was a pushover. He had to work to get every one of them on me. And all the time I was being so helpful. 'Me help!' I kept saying. 'Me do it!' I could feel His frustration bubbling nearer and nearer to boiling point with each inept attempt I made.

But He knew He couldn't do a thing. I was doing my best. I was trying to do it myself. For me it was all part of the learning process.

And if He did what I knew He was increasingly desperate to do; if He grabbed hold of me and crammed me into one of the garments with a shriek of, 'Oh, for God's sake! Let me do that, you little bugger!' . . . Well, he could have set back my development by months and months, couldn't he?

Somehow He managed to restrain Himself as, garment by agonizing garment, He finally got me stuffed into all of them. When He'd finished, I looked like a well-lagged hot water tank with a woolly hat on top.

And then came the wellies.

Oh, wellies . . . There is an entire book to be written on wellies, and on the opportunities they offer to Little Sods for parental frazzling.

There is something inherently beautiful in the design of the humble welly. It's that semi-rigidity, the way it bends between leg and foot, the way it is impossible for a sock-wrapped infant foot to slide straight into it.

Pulling tiny wellies on to an immobile foot would be hard enough, but when you've got a Little Sod tensing and untensing its toes, alternately bending them and splaying them, earnestly murmuring all the while, 'Me help! Me do it!', the task becomes well-nigh impossible.

It's wonderful. There are so many variations you can play. You start by putting the wellies on the wrong feet. Get that sorted, and you immediately try putting them on back to front. Once the correct foot is being pointed in the correct direction into the correct boot, you can shove it in forcibly, so that it jams halfway down. You then try walking around, wellies flapping out sideways like a seal's flippers. (It's quite easy – and a good idea – to fall over at this point and bang your head on something. A good screaming fit will only add to the suppressed parental fury.)

Well, I did the lot this morning. I swear it took Him as long to get the wellies on as it had all the rest of my clothes together.

But finally He'd achieved it. I was dressed. I stood in the hall like a tiny Michelin man.

I waited till He'd picked up the sledge and was reaching to open the front door, before I produced my next, carefully planned bombshell.

'Need Pee,' I said. 'Do Pee.'

He didn't actually say anything out loud, but I've got pretty good at lipreading over the past couple of years. I'd tell you exactly what He was saying, except that this book is aimed at a family audience . . .

Need
Pee

Getting me undressed again took almost as long as the dressing had. But He had no alternative. I was being good and responsible, you see. The point with Trainer Pants is that you have to say when you want to do a Pee or a Poo, and I'd done just that. It is then down to the attendant parent to see that your clothes get removed in time.

After I'd done my Pee, deciding He couldn't cope with the same thing happening again, He put a nappy on me. I protested about this. I was grownup. I could manage with Trainer Pants. 'No nappy, no nappy,' I objected strongly.

But He was deaf to my pleas. By now, a strange, demented look had come into His eyes. As He laboriously re-dressed me, layer by painful layer, He breathed more and more heavily, until His breath was coming out in barely disguised snarls.

I didn't make it any easier for Him than I had done the first time.

And the wellies took even longer this time round.

Eventually, the task was completed. He opened the door and ushered me out. Then He put the sledge on to the snow and sat me on it.

I waited until He'd pulled me to the end of the garden path. As He turned left on to the road, I neatly swayed sideways and toppled off the sledge.

I was so well padded that the fall didn't hurt at all. But He wasn't to know that. I immediately let out a bellow of pain and bawled, 'Cold! Cold!'

I refused to be comforted. He tried to get me back on the sledge, but I went into Basic Beanbag Mode (all floppy, no muscles in any of my joints) and fell off again. My screaming redoubled.

'You want to go out in the snow,' He tried telling me. 'You'll have a nice time in the snow.'

Yes, I'm sure I will. But not today. Today is going to be devoted to Him getting me dressed and undressed.

He didn't last very long. Already my cries had drawn the attention of curious neighbours. And Her face had appeared at an upstairs window. 'What on earth are you doing to that child?' She asked.

He quickly gave up. He took me back inside, and spent another hour getting me undressed.

When I was finally back in my indoor clothes again, I looked wistfully out of the window. 'Want snow!' I said. 'Want snow!'

DAY 17

To and fro . . . to and fro . . .

Let me tell you, life hasn't got a lot more interesting recently. Still, I suppose I am growing. In fact, that's all there is to do down here.

I'm now about 16 centimetres long. So what is that – about as big as a kingsize Mars Bar? Yes, probably. Different shape, though. My head's still much too big for my body.

And I'm not covered in chocolate. At the moment I'm covered in downy hair, all over everywhere. Not so keen on that. I don't want to go around looking like a furry tadpole.

Mind you, I suppose I could clean up at auditions for sci-fi movies.

DAY 24

She's very keen on the idea of my using the loo as soon
as possible. So, before She went to work this morning
I did use it . . . as a cat jacuzzi.

It's dead simple. You just put the cat in, and pull
the handle.

She didn't seem very pleased about what I'd done,
though.

Nor did the cat. Tee-hee.

DAY 26

*A couple more advances on the developmental front. I've
now got the beginnings of fingernails and toenails. Very
classy, eh? And the old eyebrows and eyelashes are beginning to grow. I suppose I could practise fluttering my
eyelashes – there's a thought . . . Bit daft, though. There's
no one down here to flutter them at.*

*That's the worst bit, being on your own with nothing to
do, just going to and fro . . . Maybe this stage of life's more
fun if you're a twin . . . or a triplet . . . or a quadruplet . . .
or one of those other combinations that get big sponsorship
deals from the tabloids.*

*On the other hand, there's not much room for me in
here. I'm not sure that I fancy playing Sardines with
anyone else.*

Of course, with there just being me, there's no competition. When I finally do emerge, I'll have the undivided attention of two parents who have no one else to lavish all their affection on. Probably better being on my own.

Ho-hum. Here we go again . . .

To and fro . . .

DAY 28

She is still maintaining this fiction that She's having another baby. Oh dear, oh dear. She's in a world of Her own. She ought to go to one of Her medical books and read up about Phantom Pregnancy.

As if She's got time for *another* baby. She's hardly got time for me. She already finds it difficult to give me all the care and attention I demand. She certainly hasn't got any energy left to spare for anyone else.

Twenty-Seventh Month

DAY 3

During the day I can now be quite reliable with the old Trainer Pants . . . when I feel like it.

I can also sometimes use the lavatory instead of the pot . . . with varying degrees of accuracy . . . again when I feel like it.

I didn't feel like doing either today. She had got me really annoyed with the way She keeps going on about having a New Baby. I know it's just Her fantasy – at least, I hope it is – but it's really beginning to get up my nose.

She was cooing away, 'Oh, won't it be lovely when you've got a nice little baby brother or sister to play with. You'd like that, wouldn't you?'

No, I wouldn't. I can't think of anything more repellent. Anyway, it's not going to happen. It's bad enough all this nonsense about Her being back at work. The idea of Her having another baby is just ridiculous.

But She went on about it, so to make Her shut up I did a great big Poo in my Trainer Pants.

And do you know what She said? She said, 'Oh dear. Have you had an accident then?'

I wish She'd stop using that expression. Why can't She get the point?

There is nothing 'accidental' about when I choose to do a Poo.

DAY 10

To and fro . .

This is a bit more fun now. When I kick out, I get a definite reaction from the Camper Van. She's very excited about it, and keeps whipping Her skirt up, trying to get Him to watch Her stomach and see the movements I make. He doesn't seem that interested. Her whipping Her skirt up seems to prompt very different thoughts in Him . . .

DAY 12

I got a new word today. Until now, whenever I've seen a traffic light at red, I've always thought it was called a 'red light'.

Now I know better. My dad was driving me to the supermarket today and just as we were coming up to the lights, they turned red. He looked up at them, and said, 'Bollocks!'

So now I know. In future, every time I see a red light, I will say, 'Bollocks!'

DAY 15

You know, my mum is absolutely obsessed by things lavatorial. Every day, first thing She asks the Juggernaut when She gets in from work is, 'And how dry were we today? How many Pees? How many Poos?'

I ask you, is that a healthy interest for a grown woman?

DAY	PEES	POOS
Monday	⦸⦸⦸⦸ ⑤	⦸⦸⦸⦸ ⦸⦸⦸⦸ ||| ⑬

DAY 17

Today She came back from work with a new bit of equipment, which She was obviously very proud of.

It's a little lavatory seat that fits on top of the big lavatory seat, and it's meant to make me feel more comfortable about using the lavatory rather than the potty.

Really! I will not be patronized in this way!

She couldn't wait to try me out on Her new toy. She assembled them both and then sat me down.

'There,' She chuckled. 'You're quite safe and comfy, aren't you? And I can leave you on your own if I want to, can't I? 'Cause you couldn't fall down that little hole, could you?'

She seemed to find the idea a lot funnier than I did.

Anyway, just at that moment the phone rang, so She did leave me sitting on it.

I expressed my opinion of the new contraption by producing a particularly nasty Poo.

And I managed to make it miss both the hole in the child lavatory seat and the hole in the adult lavatory seat.

I've often questioned the wisdom of their having had carpet laid in that room.

DAY 18

I'm quite big now. 25 centimetres actually (that's about 10 inches for those of you who never could work out the metric system). Think in terms of a litre-size bottle of washing-up liquid, and you won't be far off the mark.

My muscles are getting stronger too. That certainly helps on the old kicking front.

To and fro . . . And a KICK! And another KICK!

DAY 20

My parents keep trying to get me to show off and do my latest party trick when they have guests, but they don't like me doing the party trick I'm really best at.

That's Bottom-talking. My dad calls it 'farting', but the word doesn't begin to encompass the variety and subtlety with which a true artist like me can make a Bottom talk.

I'm also very good at choosing the perfect moment for a *bon mot* from the nether regions. Usually it's when they've got guests who they're not particularly at ease with. I wait till there's a long, awkward silence, and then break it with a real fruity one.

The trouble is, my parents think it's quite funny, and have difficulty in stopping themselves laughing.

I usually wait a moment, till they think they've got control of themselves again, and then come in with a real spluttery one.

That never fails. Always has them rolling on the floor.

DAY 22

A bit of a disaster at lunchtime today. The Juggernaut went to the freezer as usual to get something out to defrost for me. 'You'll like this,' she said, looking at the label. 'Nice lamb stew.'

Perhaps I should explain about our freezer. It's like the freezer of any other family with a two-year-old. In other words, as well as all the usual packets of frozen meat, fruit, vegetables, etc., it contains lots of yoghurt pots, twists of kitchen foil and clingfilm-wrapped lumps which are all little bits of meals long past.

What happens is, a meal comes to an end and there's a bit left. And She says, 'Ooh, that's enough for another nice meal for you, isn't it?' So She slams the remains into a yoghurt pot, or She wraps it in foil or clingfilm, and bungs it in the freezer.

Which is fine – or would be – if She had any concept of cataloguing. There are labels near the freezer, but they're used for sticking messages on the fridge.

No, I'm afraid the freezer contents in our house are just like the videos. 'This one says *EastEnders* on it,' my dad will say cautiously, as He riffles through the pile of cassettes by the television. 'So does that mean it actually *is EastEnders*?'

'No,' She will reply. 'That's the one I recorded the end of *The Sound of Music* over, followed by that documentary about babies learning to swim at three months.'

'Oh well, I can record over it then, can I?' He asks.

'Yes,' she replies, then has second thoughts. 'Better just play a bit to be sure.'

So He shoves the cassette in the slot, and plays a bit. Sure enough, it turns out to be the England–Scotland Rugby match from three years previously, with a *Tom and Jerry* cartoon recorded over the middle.

Well, when it comes to defrosting meals, She will open the freezer, riffle through the contents and pick up an icy, foil-covered, turd-shaped object. 'Now . . .' She will say tentatively, 'this is either a bit of that chicken pie you liked . . . or some of that jam sponge you had at Christmas . . . or what was left of the spaghetti we had the day the washing machine broke down . . .'

I sometimes think there's the basis of a good television panel game in this. A panel of celebrities are assembled. Something wrapped up in foil is taken out of one of their freezers, and all the others have to try and guess whose it's from and what's in it. At the end they could heat it up and whoever was right would have to eat it.

I wonder if *Celebrity Freezers* would catch on . . . ? Would it strike a chord with the viewing public? Or is it only my mum who's so incompetent when it comes to labelling the contents of Her freezer?

Oh, I almost forgot . . . The point of today's story was that the 'nice lamb stew' the Juggernaut got out of the freezer and cooked for my lunch . . . turned out to be a fish-head that had been put aside for the cat.

DAY 24

I had a haircut today, and it's the first time I've had it done exactly the way *I* wanted it. There's a kind of scalloped look to the fringe, an effect at the back rather like an advanced case of mange, and the right side's completely bald.

Well, it serves Mum right for leaving her nail scissors lying around.

DAY 25

To and fro . . . KICK! And another KICK!

DAY 26

The Crybaby was round again today and I cut its hair too. It cried.

I don't know why. The bit I cut out of its ear wasn't very big.

DAY 27

Gooey came out of the washing machine today with one of his legs missing. The material is getting so thin, he's just disintegrating. Is there any mileage in insisting he gets emergency hospital treatment? I wonder . . .

DAY 29

She is such a victim of advertising. I still wear nappies at night. (Obviously I could be dry right through, but I just choose not to be.) Anyway, She came back with some new ones today.

She'd heard them advertised on the radio. Apparently, they have 'failure-free grip-strips'.

'Failure-free'? Now that's what I call a challenge.

It's like the shampoo in the bathroom called 'No More Tears'. Hah!

DAY 30

Managed to prove that no nappy is 'failure-free', where I'm concerned.

Also confounded the claim for 'No More Tears' by doing a terrific Gazza impression throughout my entire bath routine.

Two challenges in one day.

Sometimes I surprise even myself.

DAY 31

KICK!

I'm getting seriously bored with this.

Still, I suppose I must think of the Greater Good. Think of the benefits I will be bringing to humankind. Or at least to two of them. My parents.

It's rather heart-warming to think how my arrival will transform their drab lives. They've been lonely all these years, just the two of them. And, in a little while, suddenly they'll have me! Their first baby.

How their lives will be transformed. Suddenly there will be three of us.

Twenty-Eighth Month

DAY 5

Saturday. It's great being able to move about faster. This morning She was out in the garden hanging up clothes, and I did something I could never even have thought about three months ago.

She'd started the day by cooking some kind of disgusting fruit trifle thing, all covered in cream and gunk. And when she went out to hang up the washing She put it on the kitchen dresser, just above where the cat was asleep in its basket.

Well, I'm sorry, but the sight of those two things together – fruit trifle, cat – cat, fruit trifle – was more than I could resist. In one movement – one neat flip – I managed to push the fruit trifle to the edge of the dresser, watch it topple, turn delicately in mid-air, and land – splop! – straight on top of the sleeping moggy.

Then – and this is the bit I couldn't have done three months ago – I hared out of the kitchen and was sitting on the sofa reading one of those 'educational' books She keeps trying to force down my throat, before the cat's appalled screech had finished.

The noise brought Her thundering in from the garden, and I heard another yowl as the cat was whisked up into Her arms. Immediately She appears in the sitting room doorway, fruit trifle-bespattered cat in Her arms, fully prepared to let rip at me.

I look up mildly from my book, with the slightly pained expression of an earnest scholar whose reading has been interrupted. It has the desired effect.

She turns the beam of Her fury on to the cat. 'You're wicked,' She screams, and gives its bottom a great whack. As it shoots out of Her arms, and I hear the clatter of its jet-propelled exit through the cat-flap, She calls after it, 'I'll get my own back on you, you disgusting animal!'

A very satisfactory morning's work, from my point of view. But, dear oh dear, that 'educational' book was *so* boring.

DAY 6

The cat still hasn't come back after its disgrace over the fruit trifle. Tee-hee.

I noticed this afternoon – it's become increasingly difficult to sit on Her lap. She's getting a proper pot on Her. Really, you'd have thought She'd do something about it. There's enough in the papers and on television about dieting and Weight Watchers and all that stuff.

But no, She just seems to be getting bigger and bigger. She hasn't got much lap left now. I keep slipping off. It's very annoying.

DAY 7

Still no cat. Hooray. I think I may have seen it off for good this time.

The Mystery of the Disappearing Lap took on a new dimension this evening. She'd just got back from work, and I was determined to get some of that Quality Time She waffles on about so much, so I clambered up on what's left of Her lap for a quick cuddle.

And then . . . the strangest thing happened . . .

Oy! There's something heavy pressing on the walls of my house. Still, a well-aimed kick should get rid of that! There!

I felt a definite thump from inside Her stomach! I was so surprised, I slipped off her lap again.

Thinking I may have been mistaken, I clambered back up.

Oy! I felt it again! Take that – whatever you are!

It happened again. Another definite thump.

Ugh. There is something alive inside my mum's stomach!

Suddenly, I realized what had happened. She has made good Her threat about getting Her own back.

My mum has eaten the cat!

DAY 11

You know, I have been described as heartless, but I'm not. Any behaviour of mine that appears cruel is always prompted by the highest of motives. I may sometimes do nasty things to my parents, but it's always for their own good. They need keeping in line; they must never be allowed to get above themselves.

No, deep down, I am a profoundly sensitive creature. Today I was almost sentimental – and towards one of the most unlikely recipients of anyone's sympathy: the Juggernaut. I really feel sorry for her. Next month, you see, my mum, having finally seen the error of Her ways, is giving up work. She is coming back to where She should have been all the time – at home, devoting Herself full-time to my welfare.

And where will my mum's return leave the poor old Juggernaut? Never the most attractive of women, never one who seemed likely to have much of a life, for a few brief months fortune smiled on her. Her drab existence was touched with the magic of being in almost daily contact with *me*.

It is heartbreaking to realize that her relatively young life has already known its greatest moment.

Aah. Spare a tear for the poor old Juggernaut. How will she face each dull, depressing morning, without the prospect of seeing me later in the day? There are many private tragedies which are destined to be played out unseen. Hers is one of them.

DAY 18

Gooey came out of the washing machine today with another leg missing. Now even the Chief Frog Expert at the Natural History Museum wouldn't be able to tell that he was once a frog. Realize I've left it too late to make a huge fuss over his condition, but consoled myself by bandaging him with the contents of an entire loo roll.

DAY 19

My parents had a rather worrying conversation this evening. They used a dirty word. It was 'Playgroup'.

She said, 'We really ought to get this Playgroup sorted out as soon as possible.'

'OK,' He said. 'Well, you just have to ring around, don't you?'

'Good Lord, no. There's much more to it than that. The best ones are very sniffy about who they take.'

'Really? Oh, I'm sure it'll be all right. Chap at work was talking about one he said was quite good. "Tinkerbell's", I think it was . . .'

'"Tinkerbell's"!' She echoed. 'I assume you're joking.'

'Why?'

'To get a toddler into Tinkerbell's you have virtually to put its name down five years before it's born, provide your family history going back seven generations, and give the names of three referees, including a High Court Judge and a member of the Royal Family.'

'Oh well,' He said. 'Forget Tinkerbell's.'

And forget the rest of them, as far as I'm concerned.

But I don't like the way their thoughts seem to be moving.

DAY 20

I wonder what nationality I am . . . ?
  It's interesting, wondering where one's going to be born.
  I quite fancy Japan . .
  Or maybe Papua New Guinea . . .

DAY 22

This evening She was on about trying to get me to draw. Out came the crayons and lots of paper.

I couldn't think why She'd suddenly had this rush of blood to the head on the subject, until She casually mentioned to Him who She'd had lunch with. It was the mother of Baby Einstein, which explained everything.

This ghastly little specimen has clearly started showing a talent for drawing (as well as all the other ones like walking, talking, reading and, no doubt, nuclear physics). Apparently, the little horror has drawn something absolutely brilliant – probably knocked up a version of the Mona Lisa so authentic that its parents had to tear it up in case it got into the hands of international art thieves who might have been tempted to replace the real thing with it.

Hence the sudden urgency to get me drawing.

Huh. If there's one thing my parents ought to know by now, it's that I don't respond to blackmail.

So I did my usual crayon routine – pressing down too hard so that I broke a good few of them, producing meaningless scribbles and (most important of all) making sure the paper slipped so that most of my scribbles went all over the surface of the dining-room table.

When I'd finished, He picked up one of my pieces of paper. 'Oh dear, not a budding Picasso, I'm afraid. I don't think you're ever going to produce anything genuinely artistic.'

Just you wait, I thought. One day I'll show you.

DAY 26

Saturday morning, and She wanted a lie-in. This happens far too often these days. She's out at work all week when She should be looking after me, and then at the weekends She skives off in bed. Where's this Quality Time I'm supposed to be getting?

At the moment all I get from Her is extremely low Quality Time. She's always tired or bad-tempered or Her back aches.

Anyway, I reckoned this morning if She was going to laze about in bed, then She could jolly well have me in there with Her. She could read me some stories. Well, when I say 'some' stories, I really mean 'a' story. I've got this one story I'm really hooked on at the moment. It's about a little rabbit who goes on a bus.

And the great thing about the story is – it never changes. It's not like Children's Television. In Children's Television different things happen every time . . . OK, not very different, but a bit different. Whereas in a book, every time you read it, exactly the same thing happens.

And if you enjoy the things that happen – like, say, a rabbit getting on a bus at the beginning and a rabbit getting off the bus at the end – then you can enjoy them again every time you hear it.

I don't think She likes the story about the rabbit on the bus very much. She's been going off it for the past couple of months – ever since it's been my favourite book, in fact – and this morning She really got quite shirty about it. She had only read it to me seven times and I'd just said, 'More rabbit!', when She let out a scream of 'No, I can't stand any more of it!'

Then She leapt out of bed, opened the window, and shouted down to my dad, 'I cannot stand this little monster any more!' (I thought that was a bit unfair. The rabbit in the story is a nice rabbit.) 'It's your turn to be a bloody parent!'

'But I'm cleaning the car,' came the aggrieved wail from down below. Cleaning the car is a bit of a Saturday-morning ritual with Him. He really cares about that vehicle. If He's sometimes a bit of a dead loss as a parent, it's only because I'm the wrong species for Him. If I were a car – ideally a gleaming blue car like the one He's got now – I'd have no complaints about how He treated me.

'Well, you can bloody well have some help cleaning the car!' She bellowed down at Him.

With bad grace, He came upstairs to fetch me, and then He took me out to the front of the house with the pushalong car someone had given me. It's one of those big ones with a handle at the back like a trolley which is meant to help toddlers who are learning to walk. I don't need it for that these days, but I still enjoy pushing it along.

I reckon He thought that if I had a car to play with, then He could get back to playing with His.

But there's only one fun thing to do when you're playing with a car, isn't there? And that's hitting another car with it. How else do you explain the popularity of Grand Prix racing?

So I started vrooming my car back and forth, ramming it into the front panel of His car. He was round the other side, and it took Him a minute or two to notice what I was doing. He came storming round like a demented bumblebee and snatched my car away from me.

I looked up at Him with a winning smile and said, 'Help Dad! Help Dad!'

Grudgingly, He gave me a little bit of rag like His and showed me where the bucket of water was.

I put my bit of rag in to get it wet, but somehow managed to pull the bucket of water all over myself.

After He'd got me changed into dry clothes and put my wellies on (see p. 8 for how much fun that can be), He took me out to the car again. (He'd tried to palm me off on Her again, but She wasn't having any. She didn't even rise to the bribe when He offered to get an Indian takeaway so She didn't have to cook that evening – there's no doubt about it, She really does not like that little rabbit on the bus.)

'Now you just watch Daddy,' He said firmly.

'Help Dad. Help Dad,' I said again, with my winningest smile.

'*Watch* Daddy!' He snarled.

I did for a moment or two, but seeing someone putting a fine wax finish on a bit of blue metal is dead boring. Anyway, I really wanted to help. So I picked up my little bit of rag, and went round the other side of the car to bring a fine finish to that too.

I was very pleased with the results. I think my rag

must have picked up some nice little bits of grit while it was lying on the ground, because with each sweep I made, an attractive swirly design of white lines came out on the blue of the paintwork.

I was getting quite carried away, when I suddenly heard a bellow from above me.

'WHAT THE HELL DO YOU THINK YOU'RE DOING!!!!'

I looked up at Him with an engaging smile. I was doing exactly what He had asked for a couple of days before. I was producing something genuinely artistic.

He didn't see it that way. Indeed, He was shouting so loudly that my mum had to give up Her hopes of a lie-in and come down to rescue me.

Is it the fate of all great artists to be misunderstood? I wonder if the infant Michelangelo had this trouble . . . ? Hmm, thinking of him, maybe I should have a go at a ceiling soon. My range with a well-flung bowl of food is improving daily.

Twenty-Ninth Month

DAY 9

Coo. I've got this funny stuff all over me now. It's sort of greasy and a bit like cheese. Yeugh. I don't care for it much, I must say. Actually, tonight the Camper Van had the book on pregnancy out – you know, checking my progress in the Workshop Manual – and She was talking to Him about this stuff. She said, 'The Baby'll be covered in vernix now.'

'Vernix'? Sounds disgusting, doesn't it? Like something you put down to get rid of rats.

Incidentally, I've got a lot more hair on my head now – and, thank goodness, that downy stuff has gone from most of my body. I'm quite proud of my fine head of hair, actually. Could look rather sexy – if it wasn't all gunged-up with vernix.

And you'll be glad to know that my subcutaneous fat is building up a treat.

Ho-hum. Here we go again . . .

To and fro . . . and KICK!

Ooh, that one really stopped Her in Her tracks. I am getting quite strong now, you know.

DAY 12

Gooey came out of the washing machine today without any arms.

He now looks like a scrap of dishcloth.

I am more devoted to him than ever.

DAY 15

Hooray, hooray! The day has finally come! She has returned to devote Herself to caring for me full-time.

No more Juggernaut. No more of this nonsensical talk about me going to Playgroup.

It has to be said that the new regime didn't get off to a very good start. This evening, at Her normal coming-home time, I was expecting an elaborate cuddle from Her and a speech of apology about how She should have given up work earlier. Instead, I get put to bed by Him, in His usual grumpy, perfunctory way. 'Your mum's gone to have a drink with the girls,' He said. 'Last chance to let Her hair down before the New Baby comes.'

I do wish they'd stop this stuff about the New Baby. They're just finding excuses. My mum feels so guilty about all the time She's left me with the Juggernaut that She's made up this New Baby cover story.

She got back very late. I was woken up at about midnight by noise from downstairs. It was Her singing!

I was pretty shocked. But don't worry. Now She's back looking after me full-time, I'll soon get Her behaviour back to what it should be.

DAY 16

She didn't get up till nearly noon today. Really!

Claimed She was very tired. Hungover, more likely.

And She left me for most of the day in the care of the Juggernaut. I suppose one changeover day is permissible. But She'd better get back to Her duties tomorrow.

I didn't make a scene, and I must say the Juggernaut was very good about it. Though she must've been in agony inside at the prospect of not seeing me again, she managed to maintain a brave front. No sign of tears at all.

But she did make a mistake when she was leaving. ''Bye, 'bye,' she said. 'See you tomorrow.'

Oh dear. The poor girl mustn't be allowed to foster these illusions.

'No,' I said firmly. 'No see.'

She still couldn't take it on board, poor sucker. Indeed she breezed off with hardly a backward glance at the person who has brought so much joy into her sad life over the last months.

It'll end in tears.

DAY 19

The Juggernaut came back again this morning! And my mum's still talking this nonsense about me going to Playgroup soon! *And* She keeps maundering on about the New Baby!

What is going on here?

DAY 21

She is definitely going round the twist. There's no question about it.

For example, this afternoon She was up in my room, going through the cupboard where all the clothes I've grown out of have been put away. She kept picking up these grotty old things, looking at them and saying, 'Ooh, that'll come in useful.'

This is totally daft. I don't fit into any of them. You'd think She'd have noticed that over the last couple of years I have got bigger and bigger. I mean, I know She's not very bright, nor the most observant of creatures, but it has been difficult to miss the fact. I am now a toddler, nearly two and a half years old. There's no way (even if I'd allow myself to be seen dead in them, which I wouldn't) that I'm going to fit into a newborn-size Babygro. But She kept taking this stuff out, folding it up, sorting it into piles.

Eventually, I got an explanation of what was going on in Her poor demented brain. She said, 'Look at all these lovely clothes for the New Baby.'

Oh dear. People like Her can be helped.

DAY 22

Another example today of Her increasingly serious mental condition.

She was having a rest this afternoon. (She seems far

too keen on having rests since She's been home. Doesn't She know She should be making up for lost time and spending every waking hour entertaining me?) It wasn't a sleeping kind of rest, though, just watching the box with the Juggernaut and me. Now She's back home all day, I don't think it'll be long before She's as hooked on Australian soaps as we are.

Anyway, after it finished (with a real nail-biting cliffhanger about whether someone was going to find out about someone else having kissed another someone else) She did something more peculiar. She put a CD in the CD player and plugged in the headphones.

That wasn't the peculiar bit. It was what She did next. Ooh, it was really disgusting. She pulled up Her jumper and pulled down Her skirt to reveal this great big pot belly She's got. And, as if that wasn't bad enough, She then clamped the headphones over Her tummy!

I wasn't the only one who thought this was peculiar. The Juggernaut was giving Her very old-fashioned looks by now.

'I've read this book . . .' my mum explained. (Quite honestly, given all the stupid ideas She's picked up off the printed page, I think books should be banned in our house . . . except for the one about the rabbit who gets on the bus, obviously.)

'And in this book,' She went on, 'it says that the baby in the womb is receptive to outside sounds and influences, and that you can develop a baby's musical appreciation from the prenatal stage.'

Now I've heard it all. What a load of cobblers.

'I regret not trying it with that one . . .' She indicated me '. . . but I want everything to be of the best for the New Baby.'

For a moment I was outraged. Was the New Baby going to get better treatment than I had?

But then I remembered that the New Baby doesn't exist. You can't be jealous of a figment of someone else's imagination, can you?

You know, I may have said a few harsh things over the past year about the Juggernaut's sensitivity, but the expression with which she greeted my mum's latest idiocy was dead right. Full of contempt and derision, but also with a hint of alarm at the idea she might be dealing with a dangerous loony.

My feelings exactly.

Not that She noticed. She's in a world of Her own, that one.

'All right,' She said cheerfully. 'Let's listen to some Mozart.'

And She switched on the CD.

There I was, just lying here, dozing peacefully, when I was suddenly woken up by this terrible racket!

It's coming from very close. What on earth can it be?

Sounds like some sort of music . . . Maybe the people next door are having a party . . . ?

Actually, that's something I've never thought about before. Are there any people next door?

I've always rather assumed that the womb I'm in is a kind of one-off, the only one the Camper Van who's transporting me has got.

But maybe I've got it wrong. Maybe there are lots of them. Maybe I'm on the seventeenth floor of a high-rise block of wombs.

Not going to be much fun getting out if I am. I hope the lift's working.

This noise is dreadful!

Maybe, if I bang on the walls, they'll turn it down a bit.

There, a good THUMP on the wall! And another THUMP! And another THUMP!

She looked down at Her headphone-crested pot belly and said, 'Oh look, Baby loves Mozart. Baby's dancing in time to the music.'

Absolutely no question. She should see someone.

My banging on the wall doesn't seem to have had any effect.

The bloody music's still pounding away. It seems to be getting louder, if anything.

God, what a racket! I tell you, when I get out, whatever musical tastes I may develop in later life, there's no way I'll ever listen to this rubbish!

DAY 23

At the end of this afternoon, I really had something sprung on me. I'd had my supper and was idly rubbing banana into the cat's blanket, when She came into the kitchen, followed by the Juggernaut.

'Beth's come to say goodbye to you,' She said. ('Beth' is the Juggernaut's real name. I've always pretended I can't say it. The nearest I've managed is 'Bum'. But I don't use that very often.)

I wasn't particularly interested. I was having fun finding out whether an admixture of cat's hairs improved the taste of a banana or not, so I didn't look up, just gave a token wave and a ''Bye, 'bye'.

'No,' said my mum. 'This is a Big Goodbye. Beth's not going to be here any more. She's just been here for the last week to make the changeover easier for you. But now I'm here to look after you all the time, Beth's going off to do another job.'

That did make me look up. And do you know – the great lump was grinning all over her ugly mug! 'Yeah, going to be great, the new place,' she said. 'They've got a swimming pool. I'm living in. Got my own video and use of a car.'

Really, young women today are so materialistic!

Well, I wasn't going to make her departure any easier for her. Huffily, I turned my back and concentrated on my banana and cat's hair pie.

And do you know, it didn't seem to worry her at all! She could hardly wait to get to the front door.

'I hope you'll come back to see us from time to time,' I heard my mum call after the Juggernaut's departing form.

'I doubt it,' came the reply. 'Quite honestly, I'm up to here with the Little Sod!'

Huh. Heads will roll for this. And the first one will belong to my mum!

DAY 27

I made Her life total hell today. So . . . She thinks She can manage me on Her own, does She? We'll see about that.

All day I bawled, and screamed, and kicked, and bit, and was clingy and snivelly, and generally speaking lived up to the classic definition of the 'Terrible Twos'.

Most of it was just to make Her realize that She can't treat me like that. But some of the tears were genuine. I don't like admitting it, even to myself, but I really do miss the old Juggernaut.

65

Thirtieth Month

DAY 6

Today She lost any Brownie points She might have gained by giving up work. She took me to visit a Playgroup.

I'd thought that Her discussion with Him about Tinkerbell's had been the end of the subject. But no. Clearly She's been plotting today's expedition for weeks.

At first I thought this was all right. We were just going to have a look at these snotty little creeps. My grandparents took me to the zoo a few months back, and I thought this was going to be rather the same. Take a look at the specimens, maybe watch them feeding, have a good laugh at how like real human beings they behave, and go home.

But it soon became clear that what She was actually doing was taking me to look at this Playgroup with a view to my joining it! 'In the autumn,' She said. Whenever that is.

The whole thing took on a much more sinister aspect. The bossiness of the Helpers stopped being funny, once I realized that it might one day be directed at me. And the nasty little paint-spattered creeps in dungarees suddenly ceased to be mere exhibits. I was going to become one of them.

'There, isn't it a nice Playgroup?' She said. 'You'll have a lovely time when you come here, won't you?'

Why does She keep doing this? It's one of the basic techniques of brainwashing. The theory is that if you say the complete opposite of what someone believes in often enough, they will eventually come to change their beliefs.

Well, there's no way it's going to work with me!

(Incidentally, one good moment today. I recognized one of the toddlers at the Playgroup today. It was old Crybaby.

I stuck my finger in its eye. In a changing world, it's comforting to know that some things never fail.)

DAY 7

It suddenly struck me today, after everything She said about Tinkerbell's, that this Playgroup She's proposing to put me into must be a really downmarket one. I know I haven't had my name down for five years, I'm sure they haven't produced a seven-generation family history, and no references have changed hands, least of all from members of the Royal Family.

My parents are trying to fob me off with some second-rate Playgroup. The cheapskates!

I want to go to Tinkerbell's!

DAY 9

She gave another demonstration today of the fact that She's off Her trolley. I fell over. That's not unusual. I do it quite a bit. I'm building up speed in the old running business, and life is always full of things to trip up on.

Trouble is, now it's summer, I'm out of dungarees and into shorts, which means that when I fall over it hurts a lot more.

For example, this morning I was careering from the kitchen to the sitting room, trying to knock a few hundredths of a second off the World Kitchen-to-Sitting-Room Record, when I caught my toe on Her shopping bag, which had been carelessly left in the hall, a hazard to all would-be record-breakers.

Boomph! Splat! I go headlong, and my knees take the full impact. Needless to say, I start bellowing. This is not screaming for attention. This is the real thing. It hurt!

She comes belting down the stairs from the spare room, where She's been doing yet more decorating. (I don't know what She's playing at up there – it's not as if they ever have that many guests, anyway. And I don't think many of their friends would go for wallpaper with fluffy bunny rabbits on it.) She scoops me up in Her arms. 'Oh, did you fall over then?'

Well, of course I fell over! I don't normally spend

my life spreadeagled on the hall floor, bawling my eyes out! But it wasn't worth spelling it out. Anyway, I was crying too much. I don't know what that hall carpet's made of, but my kneecaps felt like someone had been having a go at them with an industrial sander.

She managed to piece together which bit of me was hurting. 'Did you bang your knees then?' She looked at the mutilated members. So did I, through my tears.

They were a bit disappointing. Not the wreckage of shredded flesh I'd been expecting – just a bit red.

But then She showed me how stupid She really was. 'Oh well,' She said lightly, 'Kiss it better.'

And She planted a big kiss on each red kneecap.

'Kiss it better'? I mean, what is this? What is going on? Here is an adult woman, proud owner of a whole bookcase full of medical dictionaries, childcare books, etc., regular watcher of *Casualty*, *ER* and anything else with doctors and nurses in it . . . and She thinks you can cure major injuries with a dab of saliva.

Savlon, yes, I'd buy that . . . TCP . . . Witch Hazel . . . OK, they're all remedies of proven medical efficacy. But a kiss . . . ? Where has She been for the last five hundred years while medical science has been advancing by leaps and bounds?

I do sometimes despair of Her, you know.

Still, She did partly redeem Herself. After about half an hour, when nothing She'd tried would stop me bawling, She said, 'Would some Smarties make it better?'

Finally She was talking sense. I mean, obviously, down the years, exhaustive scientific tests have proved that Smarties are of real medical value.

DAY 12

Coo. I'm really fed up now. I sleep as much as I can, but there are still great acres of time when I'm aware of things. And what I'm aware of mostly is how bored I am.

The only thing that keeps me going is the thought of the huge smiles on their faces when they see me, their first little baby.

DAY 15

'Me do it!' is still my catch-phrase. Indeed no alternative to 'Me do it!' can be considered when it comes to the ceremony of Wiping the Bum.

I am a pretty smooth operator with a toilet roll – and a generous one too. (I always thought that Andrex puppy's a bit stingy with the amount he uses.) For me, no visit to the lavatory is complete if I haven't got through a whole roll of the stuff.

DAY 18

This house is getting to be like a fortress. It is so full of safety devices. Anything that I might have a good time playing with has been removed or neutralized.

For instance, they've put socket covers on all the electrical sockets, so I can't play poking things in there. There are safety gates at the top and bottom of the stairs, so I can't practise my free-fall techniques.

They've put safety catches on all the windows (so much for bungee-jumping), and the drawers and the cupboards. They've even got safety catches that go on the fridge and the freezer.

Honestly! Are they deliberately trying to stunt my development? I am at an age when, all the childcare books agree, I am full of natural curiosity about the world around me. But how am I going to find out about the world around me if I'm not allowed to look into drawers and cupboards and fridges?

When, some years hence, I end up as a jobless statistic because I haven't got sufficient qualifications, my parents will have no one to blame but themselves. Education is meant to be a process of opening doors to people, and how can you hope to open doors when they've all got bloody safety catches on them?

They've even put non-slam doorstops on some of the doors. That's seriously going to retard my development. How can I ever hope to be a proper teenager if I haven't had practice in slamming doors?

They've put a special safety guard on the stove, so I'm denied the pleasure of reaching up and pulling saucepans full of hot food off it. And today was the final straw when He came back from work with a safety guard thing to put over the front of the video. It covers the slot where the cassette goes in. Now where am I going to put all my half-eaten sandwiches, apple cores, lolly-sticks, Playpeople limbs, etc?

My parents have turned this house into an entirely fun-free zone. They are so selfish. They don't think of anyone but themselves.

DAY 20

Today She decided I was going to play with Playdoh. Whenever She talks about Playdoh to Her right-on friends, She uses phrases like 'of great educational value' and 'helping to develop the creative potential'. She doesn't realize that Playdoh is only good for one thing – and that's for sticking into little holes and crevices.

The trouble is, as I said before, our house is now so safety-conscious there are very few little holes and crevices left. I had to content myself with sticking Playdoh in some bit of plastic tubing I found in the cupboard under the stairs.

DAY 21

I'm over 40 centimetres long now. Wouldn't like to meet me on a dark night, would you?

DAY 25

Gooey had shrunk even more when he came out of the washing machine today. The smaller he gets, the more devoted to him I am.

DAY 26

Parents are funny, you know. I mean, the things they think are important about growing up are so weird. I'd have thought the basic things that count with a child are that it's healthy and . . . Well, that's about it, really. So long as it's healthy, not much else matters.

Not parents, though. Oh yes, they want you to be healthy, but that becomes almost a detail, compared to all the other things they want you to be.

I'm talking about manners here. Parents are absolutely obsessed with manners. They're terrified that their children are going to do things that will show them to be 'badly brought-up' or, even worse, 'common'. Because that would reflect on some failing in them, the parents.

The trouble is, most of the things they don't want you to do are things that are really enjoyable *to* do. Bottom-talking's one, obviously, but the other three that get my parents going most when I do them are: Thumb-sucking, Nail-biting and Nose-picking.

I can't see anything wrong with any of them.

In fact, I can see positive benefits in all of them.

Thumb-sucking is very comforting, and you don't have to be a professor of Freudian psychology to work out why. In the tiny infant mind, the thumb represents SOMETHING ELSE. You suck your thumb because it reminds you of the soothing feeling of HAVING A NIPPLE IN YOUR MOUTH.

Which renders it all the more ridiculous that She makes a fuss about me doing it. If every time I got the urge to suck my thumb I didn't suck my thumb, then I'd want a real nipple instead. And that would have been extremely inconvenient for Her when She tried to pick up Her career again, wouldn't it? Business executives tend to notice if someone in a meeting's got a baby dangling from one breast.

I would have thought that it was in Her interests for me to keep sucking my thumb for as long as possible.

Nail-biting is another thing my parents have no right to make a fuss about. They know how difficult it is to cut a baby's tiny nails; I've heard them complaining about it often enough. And yet, when I offer them a little practical help – my own personal self-trimming service – what thanks do I get? None at all.

Also, they don't seem to recognize the fact that what

I bite off and eat is very nutritious. And that I'm still supple enough to do my toenails too.

Then there's Nose-picking . . .

Well, with this I really cannot see the objection at all. Nose-picking is an entirely natural human instinct. Everyone's had that feeling of a little tickle up the nostrils, and everyone knows how irritating it can be. So what is more sensible than to alleviate that tickle by using the tool nature provided you with? Except for the undoubted pleasure – and indeed nourishment – they provide for nail-biters, why else were we equipped with fingernails?

There is nothing more pleasant than poking around in a nostril with a finger in search of the errant bogey. It offers all of the thrill of hunting, with none of the guilt about hurting our fellow creatures. A bogey does not have any independent life; it is a detached part of oneself, so it cannot be hurt.

And, in the ideal situation, since the bogey, once captured, is immediately placed in the mouth and swallowed, nothing is done to harm the food chain. Nose-picking is an ecologically perfect form of entertainment and sustenance.

I could go into great detail about the finer points of the game – about the special skills required for Nose-picking while suffering from a cold, the delicate fingernail control necessary when the snot is really crusted in, the optimum technique for flicking a detached bogey into the face of a passing parent, the

varied textures and flavours of different bogies when put in the mouth and eaten – but this is probably not the place for such refinements.

DAY 27

A bit of a chill in the house today between Her and Him. Months ago He'd fixed to go off for a weekend by the sea with some friends from the office. He says it's a break for them to work out business strategy and do a bit of snorkelling. She says it's an excuse for them to spend a whole weekend in the pub.

She also reckons He's extraordinarily selfish to leave Her 'when I'm in this condition – and I've got the little bugger to look after on my own!'

But it didn't stop Him. He was determined to go off on His jaunt and He went.

I've just realized that by 'the little bugger' She meant me. She's so rude.

DAY 29

An even deeper chill between my parents this evening. She was in a filthy mood after having to look after me all weekend.

And He came back from His jaunt by the seaside in an even filthier mood. Apparently snorkelling is quite difficult when your snorkel's gunged up with Playdoh.

Thirty-First Month

DAY 3

She really does look a bit sad these days. It's hot, and She's got so fat that She has to drag Herself around the place. I almost feel sorry for Her.

There. I've said it. You all think I'm completely inhuman and that my only aim is to make my parents' lives as near to hell on earth as is possible, but you underestimate the instinctive nobility of my nature. If I ever do anything which causes my parents pain, it is for their own good. If I wasn't always on hand, watching, ready to keep them in line, then we wouldn't be able to live together as a family. In every household somebody has to take that kind of responsibility, and in our family it's me.

Just to prove my point about how nice I really am, today I performed an act of pure goodness. I saw how stressed and exhausted She was looking and I did something to make Her life easier.

I stayed dry right through the night.

And it was heart-warming to see the reaction from Her that my simple gesture prompted. She came into my room this morning, dull-eyed and round-shouldered, with Her customary mumbled, 'Oh well, better get you cleaned up, I suppose.' But when She stripped off my pyjama trousers and nappy and saw the evidence – or rather lack of evidence – She was suddenly transformed.

Her eyes sparkled, Her shoulders straightened and a huge beam spread across Her poor silly face. 'Oh, what a clever, grown-up baby you are,' She cooed. 'You've been dry right through the night.'

Sometimes it's pathetic to see how little it takes to make Her happy.

DAY 4

Dry through the night again. Her response is still touchingly over-the-top. The way She goes on about my achievement, you'd think I'd found the secret of eternal life.

Just to show what a cool character I am, I also went through the whole day without a single moistening of my Trainer Pants. Every time I felt the need for a Pee or a Poo, I alerted Her in good time and deposited one or the other in the loo.

She was as impressed by my daytime trick as She had been by the night-time one. She looks at me now with a strange, awestruck wonder in Her eyes. Maybe I am the Messiah after all.

DAY 7

Still doing the dry-through-the-whole-twenty-four-hours routine.

Today She picked up an old pair of my Trainer Pants and said thoughtfully, 'Maybe I should throw these away . . . ?' She hesitated for a moment. 'No, I'll just hang on to them, to be on the safe side.'

And She put them away in the cupboard where She keeps the nappies. I peeked in while She was doing this, wondering whether She'd chucked out all the boxes of nappies, now I don't need those either.

But no. In fact, I'd say there were more boxes of nappies in there than usual. Mind you, She'd rather cocked-up Her bulk-buying. I take pretty big nappies these days – and, what's more, the ones you can pull up and down. And yet my Mother had filled the cupboard with boxes of the 'Newborn Baby' size.

She can't face the fact that I'm grown up, poor lamb.

DAY 8

I've now got a perfectly functioning human body, and what am I allowed to do with it? I'm given about as much opportunity for movement as an oven-ready chicken shrink-wrapped in plastic.

Really! It is getting very cramped in here. I can hardly move at all, just flex the odd muscle now and then. And I seem to have got stuck in a peculiar position with my head down. I'm beginning to wish there was some way out.

DAY 9

They bought me some new trousers today. 'Now you're a clever big baby and you're dry through the day, we don't have to leave room in your trousers for nappies or Trainer Pants, do we?'

So they made a big deal about getting these trousers that'd fit snugly round my bum. But since they also insisted on 'buying them big so that I'd grow into them,' I couldn't actually see that it made a lot of difference.

As She was putting me to bed tonight, She was going on yet again about the miracle of my dryness. 'Isn't it wonderful that we're out of nappies,' She cooed.

I considered saying, 'I know *I* am, but I didn't realize *you*'d still been in them,' but decided I couldn't be bothered.

Then She went on, 'It's so good that you're out of nappies before the New Baby arrives.'

DAY 12

Honestly! Nine months down here makes the life of the average goldfish appear packed with incident.

I could come out now. I'd be fine. I could cope.

Why are we waiting? Why-y are we waiting? Why-y are we wai-aiting? Why-y-y-y . . . ?

DAY 16

It's not just my mum who's round the twist, you know. Today I had a fine example of my dad's mentally challenged status.

She's getting lazier and lazier – rarely makes it downstairs till mid-morning these days, so He was supervising my breakfast. And I was having an egg.

I like having eggs, for two reasons.

One, you can bash them on the top with a spoon. In fact, they're the only things I am allowed to bash on the top with a spoon. Neither of my parents has taken kindly in the past to being bashed on the top with a spoon. Nor did Baby Einstein last time he was brought round for tea.

Two, eggs are beautifully gungy, and you can smear the yellow bit all over everything.

Anyway, this morning, my dad introduced something new into the breakfast egg routine. He made some toast, buttered it and cut it into thin strips. 'Look,' He said. 'Do you know what these are? They're soldiers. They're soldiers for you to dip into your egg.'

I thought this was a good idea. Getting the yellow bit of the egg on a soldier really extends its smearing range. Also you can flick bits off the end. This morning I got a direct hit in the cat's eye.

Later in the day I was dressing up. I'd got a little green plastic helmet on my head and this great plastic machine-gun someone gave me in my hands. (My mum disapproves of these toys. She says they encourage violence. Dad, on the other hand, is quite keen on them. And if She can't be bothered to get up, then She's in no position to impose Her right-on moral standards on me, is She?)

Anyway, I came bursting into the kitchen, where He was trying to read the paper. I pointed the machine-gun at Him, and pulled the trigger, and it made this rat-a-tat noise like I've heard on the television. (My mum also tries to stop me watching things on television that She reckons are violent, but it's a losing battle. Any two-year-old with a remote control can find someone being shot to pieces on some channel or other at most times of the day or night.)

My dad looked up from His paper and said, 'Ooh, I know what you are. You're a soldier, aren't you?'

Honestly! When I want to dress up like a strip of buttered toast, I will dress up like a strip of buttered toast.

I do worry sometimes about the genetic inheritance. I'm getting from these two.

DAY 18

Gate Fever! That's what I've got. Gate Fever's what long-term prisoners get when their release day comes near. And I'm sure my release date must be near. It must.

How near, though? I should have started making scratch-marks on the wall on Day One. Then I'd know where I stood (or floated). Too late to think of that now.

You know, prisoners who get Gate Fever go entirely potty. Well, I'm going entirely potty. Let me out! Please let me out!

DAY 19

I have given careful consideration to the possibility that there might be something in this New Baby business, but have come to the conclusion that there cannot be.

For one very simple reason.

They've got me. They don't need another baby.

Besides, they wouldn't do that to me.

She is getting massively fat, though.

DAY 22

There isn't room to swing a cat in here. Not room to swing a gerbil even. Or a shrew. In fact, you couldn't swing anything. There's absolutely no swinging room at all.

I can't stand this much longer. Something's got to give.

DAY 24

Gooey is now out of bandages, but about the size of a biscuit. I rely on him more than ever.

DAY 25

They do go on about things. She keeps telling me that
She'll soon be going away for a few days and that when
She comes back She'll have something very exciting
with Her. First time She said it I got quite interested.
I thought She meant She was going to buy me the
£249.99 Super-Mega-C D-Blaster they so shamefully
failed to give me last Christmas.

But no. The thing She described as exciting was a
New Baby. This really isn't funny any more.

DAY 26

She's moving round the house so slowly now. I've seen
elephants with more get up and go – and with slimmer
figures.

DAY 31

This is getting intolerable. I've got to do something.
Maybe, if I start putting some pressure on down
HERE . . .

Thirty-Second Month

DAY 1

I woke up this morning and had a nasty shock. I toddled
in to my parents' room, as usual, to find – my grandparents in their bed! Her mum and dad – in my parents'
bed!

Yuk. This is the kind of thing that could have a
very traumatic effect on a sensitive young psyche. Who
knows what anti-social behaviour of mine in later life
will have been caused by this unpleasant bombshell?

What was worse, both my grandparents were asleep.
With their mouths open. Snoring. Yuk. And, by my
grandfather's side of the bed, there was a set of teeth
in a glass of water. Couldn't he afford a goldfish?

I let out a huge wail of shock and horror. That woke
them up all right.

Within seconds my grandfather had swallowed the
teeth out of the glass. Perhaps it was just as well he
couldn't afford a goldfish.

Won't be long now. Can't be long now. Something's got to give. Surely?

My grandparents spent the day trying to entertain me. And pretty useless they were, let me tell you. Their hearts didn't seem to be in it. My grandmother wasn't able to concentrate at all. She kept looking at the phone all the time.

The old boy wasn't much better either. He took me to the swings, but he's a very pussy-footed pusher. I like really whizzing up in the sky, but he just pushed me gently, like I was in a Baby Bouncer. Very disappointing.

Well, here I am. After the nine months I've just been through, this had better be good!

It was late afternoon when the phone eventually rang. I was on the floor playing with the cat. (Well, 'playing' is probably not what the cat would have called it. I had one arm round its neck and was making it up with face paints. My parents wouldn't have let me do anything like that, but my grandparents were so preoccupied they didn't notice. There are some advantages in having them around.)

Apparently the telephone call was the one my grand-parents were waiting for. They made a great fuss about it. My grandmother burst into tears, and the old boy looked pretty emotional too.

'The Baby's come! The Baby's come!' my grand-mother kept telling me.

'And both Mother and Baby are fine!' She went on. As if I cared.

'Won't it be lovely!' she cooed. 'You'll have someone new to play with!'

I jabbed a face-paint stick into the cat's eye, to show what happens to people I play with.

Coo. They do cry a lot out here. The Camper Van has got tears pouring down Her face, and the drip She's with doesn't seem to be in a much better state. If this is Life, I must say so far I'm pretty underwhelmed by the whole business.

My grandparents finally got me to bed about nine. (I played up something rotten. I know my duty.) They're going to take me to the hospital tomorrow to see the New Baby.

9.15 p.m.   I'm jolly hungry. I think I'll latch on to one of those nice juicy nipples.

9.30 p.m.   Hungry again. Time for another suck.
9.45 p.m.   Still hungry. More! More!

And so on, and so on, through the rest of the night. This is me, asserting my rights of total control over Her. She's going to regret She ever opted for Demand Feeding.

DAY 2

When I woke up this morning, my dad was here as well as my grandparents. He looked really hungover. Serves Him right.

And He told me the name they've given this New Baby. I haven't stopped laughing since. Poor little brute. Tee-hee. And they say there's no justice. Tee-Hee.

I've just realized that this ridiculous word they keep saying is the name they are proposing to lumber me with for the rest of my life. They cannot be serious!

I was taken to the hospital to see the New Baby this afternoon.

What a lot of fuss about nothing. And what a joke. It's obviously a boiled ham wrapped in a blanket. Ugly little brute. My mum and dad kept trying to get me interested in it, but, with the best will in the world, what is interesting about a boiled ham?

They told me the Baby had got a present for me, and thrust this huge gift-wrapped package into my hands.

Hooray, I thought, finally they have realized the error of their ways.

It was a Thomas the Tank Engine train set. I was a bit disappointed. I mean, I suppose a Thomas the Tank Engine train set is O K, but it's not a £249.99 Super-Mega-CD-Blaster, is it?

And, as for this fiction that it was a present from the Boiled Ham . . . Well, I treated that with the contempt it deserved. I mean, the Boiled Ham can't *do* anything. I'm damned sure it couldn't have got out of its cot, pootled across to Toys 'R' Us, picked the Thomas the Tank Engine train set off the shelf, gone to the check-out, whipped out a credit card . . . I'm sorry, I just don't believe it.

My parents were terribly keen to get a photograph of the two of us together. This is very peculiar. There's something about the arrival of the Boiled Ham that has pushed my dad into photographic overdrive. The camera's permanently glued to His eye. I'm sure the Boiled Ham thinks He always has a rectangular black face with a lens for a nose and a viewfinder instead of eyes.

Anyway, He spent the whole afternoon snapping away at the lump in the blanket. I don't know why He bothered. When they come out, all the photographs will look exactly the same. Maybe He's aiming to have an avant-garde exhibition of them one day. Identical pictures, with titles like 'Boiled Ham No. 1', 'Boiled

Ham No. 2', 'Boiled Ham No. 3', etc. I can't think of any other reason why He wants to take them.

But He was terribly keen to get one of me holding the thing. So was She. 'Won't it be lovely,' She kept saying. 'You, the Big One, holding the Little One – something to treasure for the rest of your life.'

What? She has a pretty peculiar idea of my priorities if She thinks I'm going to treasure something like that.

Still, I'm a tolerant soul. If all this makes them happy, I thought, it's no skin off my nose. And, after all, it's not for long. In a couple of days, She will be back home, the Boiled Ham will be left in the hospital where it belongs, and normal life can continue again.

So I sat obediently on a chair while they picked the blanket-wrapped lump out of its cot and plonked it on my knee. I let it lie there. I didn't want more physical contact with the thing than was strictly necessary.

'Come on, you've got to hold the Little One. You don't want the Little One to fall on to the floor, do you?'

Now, there *was* a thought . . . I started to jiggle my knees, but He leapt in quickly to stop the bundle from dropping.

'Come on, put your arms round the Little One. Give a nice hug.'

Oh, all right. I closed my arms around the Boiled Ham, and squeezed.

'No, not so tight, not so tight!'

Obediently I relaxed my grip, and looked dispassionately down at the thing in my arms. It certainly didn't look like a baby. Well, not like me anyway. Not many redeeming features. Not many features at all, actually. Scrunched-up little face. I've seen more attractive prunes.

Also, it smelt. Partly, it smelt like a chemist's shop. But underlying that was another, less wholesome, aroma.

'Now,' said the camera that was His face, 'look up at Daddy and give me a nice big smile.'

No, I'm sorry. There is a limit. I'd been the model of co-operation. I'd touched the thing. I hadn't dropped it. I hadn't squeezed it too hard. There was no way I was going to smile too.

'Oh, haven't you got a solemn face?' She said.

And with reason. This was an extremely serious occasion. I saw no cause for merriment.

He snapped away, making some of the silly noises which in the past had been known to make me crack a smile, but I didn't give in. When his exhibition opens, 'Boiled Ham with Little Sod' will demonstrate a proper appreciation of the gravity of what was happening.

While this photocall was going on, She kept saying from the bed, 'Now you two are going to be such good friends, aren't you?'

What – me and the Boiled Ham? Friends? In your dreams, sweetheart.

After a while, He took me away. He kept apologizing that I couldn't stay longer, but it had already been far too long for me. On the way home, he stopped and bought me an ice cream. It was small compensation for what I had just been through.

And I soon got tired of playing with my Thomas the Tank Engine train set. My dad set it all out, and we both played with it for a few minutes. Then I realized all the train did was go round and round, so I lost interest and wandered off to pour finger paints into the cat's water bowl.

When I went back into the sitting room an hour later, He was still stretched out on the floor, playing with my Thomas the Tank Engine train set. He is such a baby.

The whole business of my mum being away is getting rather boring. I can't wait till She comes home and leaves the Boiled Ham in the hospital where it belongs.

They brought a mean-faced toddler to the hospital to pay homage to me this afternoon. Ugly little brute, a real Munchkin. They kept trying to get it to take notice of me. I can't imagine why. The Munchkin appeared to have no interest in me at all. Which is fine. The feeling's mutual.

Still, nothing to worry about. There's no reason why the two of us should ever see each other again.

DAY 3

She came home from hospital today – and actually had the nerve to bring the Boiled Ham with Her! Well, a joke's a joke, but this has gone too far.

What is going on?

He and She are incredibly interested in it, though, so I played along to humour them. But after ten minutes I got really bored. I mean, I get bored with toys after ten minutes, and they're a lot more interesting than the Boiled Ham. Toys at least make noises or flash lights when you press buttons on them. From what I've seen of it, there are no buttons on the Boiled Ham.

So, after the ten minutes, I said, 'Home now,' meaning, 'Yes, that's enough. You can take it home now.'

My parents completely misunderstood my point, just went all gooey and said, 'Yes, our new little baby's home now.'

Presumably somebody from the hospital will be along to take it back later.

So this is where they're expecting me to live, is it? Don't care much for their taste in decor, I must say. That cot with all its frills and flounces looks like something out of a cake decoration catalogue. And as for those tasteless fluffy rabbits on the wallpaper . . . yeugh! I can only hope this is temporary accommodation. It's a bit downmarket from the kind of thing I had in mind.

Also that Munchkin is here for some reason. I hope that's temporary too. Presumably it has a home to go to. Well, it had better get back there, sharpish.

Unbelievable! After my supper, She went upstairs and came down carrying . . . that Boiled Ham! This is appalling. It's still here!

Unbelievable! After my afternoon snooze, She picked me up and carried me downstairs to the sitting room where, lounging around in front of the television as though it owned the place, was . . . that nasty little Munchkin. This is appalling.

I see a potential problem. My parents have got to realize that I am the only thing of importance in their lives. I can't allow their attention to be distracted by other children.

Still, if I put in a good night's screaming my head off, that should help them see the error of their ways.

DAY 4

The Boiled Ham is staying in the spare bedroom!

I suppose I'll just have to be patient. In a couple of days She'll have lost interest in it and sent it back. That's what She did with the Aerobic Step and the Nordic Skiing Machine and most of the other stuff She's had on free approval.

Clearly my point is not getting across. Right. They've asked for it! I'll see to it they don't close their eyes for a single moment tonight!

DAY 10

I found Her in the Boiled Ham's room this morning. She was changing its nappy. Yuk. The nappy was all covered with what looked like milky coffee.

It didn't smell like milky coffee, though.

Honestly, why does She keep the thing when it's so disgusting?

DAY 17

Oh, the shame! The ignominy!

My parents have bought a double buggy! And I'm expected to sit in it, strapped up next to the Boiled Ham!

Have they any idea what effect this is going to have on my street cred?

DAY 22

We went out shopping this morning. And for reasons best known to Herself, She brought the Munchkin along too.

Why? There is something strange going on here. What unhealthy hold does the little monster have over my mum? Maybe it is in league with the devil. That would certainly explain why its face looks the way it does.

My usual supermarket mayhem was limited this morning, because She insisted on bringing the Boiled Ham with us.

What I've got into the habit of doing recently is walking around pulling things off the shelves, knocking down piles of cans, bumping into Senior Citizens' trolleys, etc. Then, when I get tired, I whinge until She picks me up and puts me in the sitting bit of her trolley. From that vantage point, I can make a wonderful mess of all the stuff She's already collected off the shelves.

But today I was prevented from following my normal routine. Rather than picking one of the trolleys with a sitting bit, She got one with a cradle bit. And She put the Boiled Ham in that.

I had to *walk* all the way round the supermarket!

What's more, I couldn't create my usual merry hell among the shelves. She has invested in a new weapon of torture, which I'm sure is forbidden under the Geneva Convention. I've seen them around, but She's never tried one on me before. It's effectively a kind of manacle, and it severely limits my range for exploration.

There's a clasp thing one end that fits on to her wrist – or one of the uprights of the trolley in the supermarket – and another clasp thing on the other end, which fits round my wrist. Between them is a curly wire.

What is She doing to me? How can I make Her realize I am not a telephone?

I went to sleep on the way back from the supermarket, and when we got home, She must've left me in the pram in the hall. That's where I woke up, anyway.

Imagine my shock at the first sound I heard. It was her reading out loud. She was actually in the sitting room, reading a book to the Munchkin! It appeared to be some feeble story about a rabbit who gets on a bus.

Well, I couldn't tolerate that, could I? So I let out an immediate bellow of fury.

Give Her Her due, She did come and fetch me instantly. But then She had the nerve to take me into the sitting room, sit down with me on the sofa next to the Munchkin, and ask, 'Would you like to listen to our nice story too?'

Would I hell? I took the only action appropriate in the circumstances. Loudly, pungently and splutteringly, I filled my nappy.

It worked. She might have pretended to ignore the noise or the spreading dampness on Her forearm, but there was no way She could ignore that smell.

Thrusting the book at the Munchkin, with a cry of 'You just have a look at that while I sort Baby's nappy out', She was upstairs changing me within seconds.

Victory for me, I think.

She went to change the Boiled Ham's nappy in the middle of my story! The rabbit had got on the bus, but it hadn't got off yet! This was intolerable!

I understood immediately. So the Boiled Ham reckoned it could get Her attention by doing a Poo in its nappy.

It was using my tactics, finely honed over the last two and a half years. Huh, I thought, two can play at that game.

Concentrating like mad, I made a tremendous effort, and managed to fill my Trainer Pants spectacularly. (Well, some of it got caught in the Trainer Pants. The rest didn't.)

I needed more than changing. I needed Industrial Cleaning.

DAY 23

Today I have declared the official end of all Toilet Training! Any advances I have made over the last two years are hereby reversed!

So there was no way I was going to go through last night dry without a nappy.

Well, I did go through it without a nappy, but I was by no means dry, and it wasn't exactly fragrant either.

I'm going to win, you know, and the sooner the Boiled Ham recognizes that, the better!

Thirty-Third Month

DAY 2

There's no two ways about it; I think they really intend to keep the Boiled Ham. They haven't said anything about sending it back where it belongs. And it's taking up almost all of their time.

Don't worry, though. This is my patch, and I won't give up an inch of it.

That Munchkin's still around! I've a nasty suspicion that my parents regard it as some kind of permanent fixture.

Yeugh. Don't worry, though. This is my territory, and the Munchkin's not going to get the tiniest part of it.

DAY 5

I had a ghastly thought this morning. What if my mum was right . . . ? If what I thought to be Her fantasy was in fact the truth . . . ? If the Boiled Ham actually *is* the New Baby She kept wittering on about . . .

. . . then that horrible little monster is my own flesh and blood. Yuk. The mind frankly boggles.

DAY 6

I had a ghastly thought this morning. Suppose the Munchkin who hangs around the house all the time actually belongs here . . . ? Suppose it's related to them in some way . . . ? Suppose – even worse thought – it's related to me in some way . . . ? Suppose – worst thought of all – it's actually my elder sibling!

Yeugh! I feel really upset by the idea. Apart from anything else, it would mean that that womb I sloshed around in cheerfully for nine months actually had a previous tenant.

When I had this thought, I was so upset that I threw up all over my cat.

DAY 8

I overheard Her talking to Him in Her worried voice this evening. The subject that was getting Her all uptight was Sibling Rivalry.

She must have consulted one of the childcare books about it, because when She came to kiss me goodnight, She said – without any subtlety at all – 'We're all going to be one big happy family, aren't we? You're not going to be jealous of the New Baby, are you?'

Well, of course I'm not. Something like that isn't

worth being jealous of. I mean, it can't do anything. It just squirms around, bawling its head off and dirtying nappies. I could feel sorry for the poor little bugger, yes, but jealous . . . ? Forget it.

Thank God I never went through a stage like that.

Mind you, She does seem to spend a disproportionate amount of time with the Boiled Ham . . . Time She should be spending with me . . .

Someone – not me, of course, I'm far too grown-up – but someone hypersensitive might start to think She was more interested in the Boiled Ham than in me . . .

Except that idea is entirely preposterous . . .

Isn't it . . . ?

DAY 10

I've just been looking through the pile of loot that the Boiled Ham's been given in the last month, and I've noticed two things.

The first is – there's not as much as there was when *I* appeared on the scene! Tee-hee!

My arrival prompted presents from everyone. Great mountains of gear there was.

Whereas, for the Boiled Ham . . . there's considerably less. The explanation is partly Present Fatigue Syndrome, and partly – which is very good news for me – Second Baby Syndrome. When I arrived, no one up until that point could have imagined that my parents – a fairly, it has to be said, unprepossessing couple – were capable of producing anything so magnificent.

But when the Boiled Ham appeared, the excitement and surprise had gone. Everyone knew my parents could have babies. They'd done it before, after all. And, of course, the Boiled Ham was nowhere near as attractive as I was. It really is an ugly little bugger, you know.

The second point I noticed about the Boiled Ham's presents is how commercialized all the gear has become. Everything the little horror's been given is a piece of merchandizing for something I've seen on television.

What kind of a world-view will all this commercial brainwashing give the poor little Boiled Ham? It'll grow up imagining that trains not only have funnels, but also faces on their fronts; that letters are delivered by men with big noses and not enough fingers; and that the world is peopled by ecologically aware animals, politically correct Native Americans and cheery hunchbacks, all of who sing so-called lyrics by Tim Rice.

I'm glad I'm not the Boiled Ham's age. You know, I don't envy the younger generation one bit.

DAY 13

I can hardly bring myself to relate what She perpetrated today. You may remember, some months ago She took me along to a Playgroup to have a look round. Well, today She took me along to enrol as an inmate!

Naturally, I started to scream as soon as I arrived. I am a fine, sensitive soul – I can't possibly be expected to mix with all that riff-raff. It might have been different if they'd sent me to join the Hooray Henrys and Henriettas at Tinkerbell's, but this lot seemed dead common.

'Don't worry,' said the Chief Helper, a huge, over-muscled girl, who could have represented Britain in the Heartiness Olympics. 'Most of them cry when they start, but they all settle down very quickly.'

Huh. As I said earlier, I know a challenge when I hear one.

'And what about toilet habits?' asked Miss Heartypants. My blood chilled. 'Use the lavatory all right, can we? Stay dry through the day?'

'Oh yes,' my mum replied breezily.

Suddenly Her eyes were alerted to the over-spill from my Trainer Pants.

I had Her absolutely undivided attention for an hour this morning. The Munchkin wasn't there. Blissful. I could do with more of this.

Mind you, it came back at lunchtime and – goodness – was it in a bad mood! Totally exhausted. It had a long sleep this afternoon, which should have meant that I had another hour of my mum's undivided attention. But unfortunately I had a long sleep too.

I had a sleep this afternoon and woke up in a filthy mood. Decided to take it out on Her.

After my sleep, I woke up in a filthy mood. Decided to take it out on Her.

DAY 14

I got all geared up to create a massive scene this morning when She tried to take me off to Playgroup, but nothing happened. She didn't take me anywhere.

I'm glad She's come round so quickly. Usually She keeps on much longer about things like that. Perhaps finally She's realized what She should have noticed from the start – namely, that I am always right.

DAY 15

What a filthy, low-down trick!

Having lulled me into a false sense of security yesterday, She had the nerve to take me to Playgroup again this morning! Apparently the idea is that I go two mornings a week.

This is an appalling assault on the rights of the individual . . . well, of me, anyway.

I screamed all morning. And, as for my toilet behaviour . . . I don't think the Playgroup Helpers have ever got through quite so many bottles of Dettox.

DAY 17

I don't think my parents are taking enough notice of me. Yes, obviously I am the person around whom the entire household revolves, but they still spend far too much time with that Munchkin. I will have to come up with something.

DAY 18

Think I've worked out a strategy. Every time I cough they come running. I'll get them worried about my health. Can't fail.

So, I've experimented with a new kind of crying. It's more piercing, and I do a bit of shaking and sobbing between yells.

I tried it early this evening for the first time.

She was reading me a story this evening – that rather entertaining one about the rabbit who got on the bus – when we suddenly heard this terrible crying sound from the Boiled Ham's bedroom. She tensed instantly, but I said, 'More 'tory! More 'tory!'

Give my mum Her due, in spite of the banshee wailing from above, She did finish the story – all the way up to that exciting moment when the rabbit gets off the bus. But the minute She'd read the last word, She shot upstairs like She had a rocket up her bum.

I was a bit worried. The noise the Boiled Ham was making was really good. It sounded like the little monster was genuinely in pain. Of course I knew it wasn't, but I was afraid She might be fooled. I fondly remembered the technique, you see, from a couple of years back.

So I snuck upstairs and lurked outside the Boiled Ham's bedroom to observe what happened.

She took Her time getting up here. Still, I could see I'd got Her worried. There was a paranoid look in Her eye.

She took me out of my cot, and I pretended I was hungry, but lost interest in the nipple as soon as it was offered, and started crying again. The new crying, of course.

She looked at me dubiously for a moment. Come on, I was urging her, this has got to be worth a consultation with the childcare book – if not a call-out to the doctor. This sounds really serious, doesn't it?

But do you know what She had the nerve to do? She picked me up, screaming though I was, and put me back in my cot. Oy, I wanted to shout, how dare you! This noise ought to have you scared witless.

But She wasn't fooled. She moved to the door and said, 'I know you're just playing me up, you wicked baby. The first one used to do just the same. I got really worried then, but this time I recognize it for what it is – sheer naughtiness. Now you go to sleep!'

And She actually went out of my room, and closed the door!

How callous can you get!

I heard what my mum said in the Boiled Ham's bedroom. When She came out, She looked down at me and said with a smile, 'There are things a second one can't get away with, you know.'

Yippee! Was I happy to hear that! The Boiled Ham's going to have to be a lot more subtle than I was.

I got away with all sorts of things by arriving first. And the Boiled Ham won't be able to! Tee-hee. Poor little sucker!

DAY 21

I've just noticed something. Because of my mean skills at nappy-filling – seeing that a lot of it trickles out or misses the nappy entirely – I go through a good few changes of clothes in the average day.

And I've just noticed that a lot of the clothes I get put in AREN'T NEW! There are one or two garments that I saw handed over as presents by people who came to pay homage to me in my first weeks, but the bulk of the stuff I'm dressed in is second-hand!

What's going on here? I'm being marginalized. My parents aren't that poor. Why should I have to put my limbs into Babygros that have been washed so much nobody can tell what colour they were when they started?

DAY 22

I got an explanation today for all those old clothes they dress me in – and it was worse than I could have believed possible.

She was just doing my seventeenth change of clothes of the day, when the Munchkin walked uninvited into my room. It looked up at me on the changing mat with its customary distaste and, as usual, I screamed at the sight of it.

But then She said to it, 'Oh, look, Baby's wearing this lovely blue and white stripey Babygro that you wore when you went for your first check-up at the clinic.'

WHAT! It's bad enough wearing hand-me-downs, but hand-me-downs from THAT creature are intolerable!

Yeugh! To think that the Munchkin's bum has soiled the garment that I am wearing . . .

Well, the least I could do was to prove my ability to soil it better than the Munchkin ever could in its wildest dreams.

It wasn't just me who had to be changed out of the alien Babygro. I managed a real wide-range scattergun attack. She and the Munchkin needed a complete change of clothes too!

They're going to have to learn to treat me with a bit more respect!

DAY 24

Mother of mine, may you be forgiven!

I was never allowed to have a dummy. Whinge as I might, She never succumbed to the easy option of shoving a bit of rubber into my mouth for me to chew on. It was Her or nothing.

Looking back, I'm quite surprised that She's got any breasts left; the way I used to nibble away at them, I'd have thought they'd have scalloped edges by now. But no, they're still there, more or less intact. Mind you, they sag a bit more than they did when I started on them. Tee-hee.

But with the Boiled Ham She's had an entirely different approach. It's such a miserable little sod, the way it cries all the time, that I can understand her thinking. The temptation to block its mouth with anything is so strong, She's given in to the dummy. Mind you, if it was left to me, I'd use something more permanent . . .

All Her principles have gone straight out of the window. And She doesn't seem to care. I heard Her saying to one of her right-on friends who took Her to task about it, 'Oh, quite honestly, I haven't got the energy these days. It's totally different with the first one. Then you don't know anything, so you come into the whole business with all these high-minded principles you've got out of books. With the second, it's a matter of survival. Anything for a quiet life.'

That made me feel rather good. Clearly I got the First Class Gold Star Service when I was a baby, while the Boiled Ham's being fobbed off with Tourist Economy.

The right-on friend was terribly disappointed. 'I never thought I'd hear you say any baby of yours had a dummy,' she said reproachfully.

'It's not a dummy,' my mum replied heatedly. 'These days it's called a "soother".'

As if that made any difference.

Very odd. She just shoved something in my mouth. It's shaped like a nipple but, although I've sucked and sucked and sucked at it as hard as I can, so far I haven't been able to get anything out of it.

Also, unlike a nipple, it doesn't seem to have the rest of Her attached to it.

Good heavens! Does She have detachable nipples?

I wonder which other parts of Her body She can unscrew and leave around. Hmm. I heard Him call from the kitchen where He was doing the washing-up this evening,

'Could you give me a hand?' Maybe her feet come off as well . . . ?

Still, it is quite nice to chew, this detachable nipple. Very soothing.

DAY 27

A new kid started at Playgroup today. It screamed its head off, and kept doing Poos in its Trainer Pants. All the rest of us thought it was terribly funny.

And the great thing was . . . it was Baby Einstein! The little horror who's supposed to have made every developmental advance in its life well ahead of me has finally been shown up for what he really is. He cries and Poos himself at Playgroup! Tee-hee, what a turn-around.

I'm, incidentally, already acknowledged as the Playgroup wit. Some of my *bons mots* have everyone falling about. And when I do Bottom-talking, they can hardly contain themselves. (Well, actually a lot of them *can't* contain themselves.)

Thirty-Fourth Month

DAY 2

One good thing about the few weeks before the Boiled Ham's arrival and the time since is that it's curbed my dad's 'tendencies' towards my mum. As ever, He's kept trying to paw away at Her, but I'm glad to say over the last few months She hasn't been feeling like any of that nonsense.

This is very good news, so far as I'm concerned. I personally don't think my parents should have a sex-life. I mean, obviously they had to do it once to achieve the apotheosis of their lives – i.e. the conception and subsequent wondrous appearance of ME – but they should have left it at that.

They certainly should have stopped before they conceived the Boiled Ham. The fact that they allowed such an appalling event to take place shows they have no sense of responsibility at all.

What my dad has got to realize is that, since I've been around, He has had absolutely no rights to my mum. She's mine, all mine.

True, at the moment, She has the Boiled Ham crawling all over her, but allowing that to happen can surely only be a temporary aberration on Her part.

Still, there have been a few signs recently that He could be getting frisky again. I've overheard muttered conversations from their bedroom which have had a distinctly lascivious tone. I've also heard mention of the significant words 'six-week check-up'.

I remember this from when I was six weeks old. She went back to the hospital for a kind of post-Baby MOT. And it was clear from the way He went on about it that this was deeply significant to Him, and it was the go-ahead for all kinds of unbridled activities.

Well, it was evident this evening, from the looks they exchanged when He came back from work, that the 'six-week check-up' had been fine. And that, having been given the green light, His sole intention was to gun away from the lights as quickly as possible.

Hmm . . . I had to do something about this.

Recently I've been getting a bit slack about my night-time routine. Oh, sure, I whinge and scream and argue about what time I get to bed, but once I'm there, after the odd token complaint, I tend to flake out pretty quickly and sleep through till the morning. You see, most days I'm utterly knackered. You've no idea how exhausting toddling is.

So I admit I've been giving my parents far too easy a night-time ride (unfortunate expression in today's particular circumstances), and generally not living up to my credentials as a fully fledged Little Sod.

Tonight, seeing that glint in my dad's eye, I was determined to revert entirely to my former night-time screaming routine. If He thought He was going to get any fulfilment that night, He'd certainly got another think coming.

So I dragged out the arguments over bedtime as long as I could, made lots of spurious demands for stories and videos and drinks of water, and when they finally got me into bed, I was determined that no way was I going to go to sleep. I'd just scream and scream until . . . ZZZZZZZZZZZZZZZZZZZZZZZZZZ . . .

There is something funny going on with my parents. He's had a very devious look in his eye over the past few days. He keeps going on about a 'six-week check-up', and then going off into rather smirky-sounding giggles.

I'm not sure what He's up to, but I don't like it.

He's also been touching Her a lot recently, in a rather intimate way. I don't like that either. Her body is my property, to do what I choose with – forever. Nobody else has even got squatting rights in it.

Whatever it is they're planning has got to be stopped.

No need for anything too elaborate. The old stand-by of screaming my head off all night should do the trick. Here goes . . .

DAY 3

Damn. I actually had to be woken up this morning.

All my cunning plans for keeping them awake all night came to nothing.

But, from the bleary, bloodshot expression in their eyes, I don't think a lot of sleeping got done last night.

And from the bad-tempered way He slammed the front door as He left for work, I don't think it was mad, unbridled passion that kept them awake.

Hmm, I wonder what's been going on . . .

I kept screaming until it was time for them to get up this morning, and then I dropped into a deep and peaceful sleep. When I woke late morning and my poor bleary mum said how angry She was at having been kept awake all night, I tried to give Her the benefit of another of my smiles. Unfortunately, it rather disintegrated into a belch. Luckily, She was totally disarmed and said it was impossible to be cross with me.

That's what you think, sunshine. I'll see to it you have every reason to question that rash assertion over the next few months. Tee-hee.

I actually heard what happened last night. She was talking to the Boiled Ham on the subject, saying how naughty it had been to keep Her and poor Daddy awake for so long.

Hey, this is brilliant. I no longer have to be a full-time contraceptive. The Boiled Ham can help me out. We can do shifts.

For a moment, a little spark of sentimentality came into my soul. I had a misty vision of me and the Boiled Ham doing other things together . . . co-operating in making our parents' lives hell . . . even – dare I say it – becoming friends . . . ?

I considered this seductive vision for a full minute before I came up with the appropriate reaction to it.

No way!

Right from the start it's been a state of war between me and the Boiled Ham. And that's how it's going to stay.

Mind you, its excesses can still be useful to me from time to time.

For instance, I'll let the Boiled Ham handle contraceptive duties again tonight. It's a wonderful feeling to know that, while you sleep, others are working on your behalf.

Bad luck, Dad.

DAY 6

I am now pretty damn good on parts of the body. I mean talking about them, not using them (though, actually, I'm quite good at using them too – just ask Her about the clever reverse backflip with which I knocked that jug of hot custard over the other week!).

But I'm referring to my language skills. I can now say the words for most bits of me. 'Nose.' 'Mouth.' 'Ear.' 'Eye.' 'Tooth.' 'Tummy.' 'Belly-Button.' 'Toe.' 'Finger' . . . and 'Fum'.

I also have my own words for more private bits of me, but you'll have to guess what those are. I'm not going to have them printed – this is not that kind of book.

True, some of my pronunciations are a bit indistinct,

and you'd need to be trained in basic Little Soddese to know what I'm talking about, but I'm getting there.

Certainly, I'm way ahead of the Boiled Ham. Its only means of communication are Screaming, Peeing, Pooing and Throwing Up. How unsophisticated.

DAY 10

They start Christmas really early at Playgroup. It's only October, and already the Helpers have got us making paperchains. Making paperchains involves painting. And painting involves lots of jars of water to knock over and paint to smear everywhere. The challenge is obviously to avoid getting any paint on the pieces of paper destined to become paperchains, but it's also to avoid getting any paint on the newspaper they put all over the tables. What you should really be aiming for is the furniture, the floor, the Helpers' clothes – particularly Miss Heartypants', and of course the faces of the other children.

I can modestly state that this morning I was bloody good at getting direct hits on all the above-mentioned targets. Some of us have got these skills and some of us haven't.

The other thing they were talking about this morning is a 'Christmas Pageant'. I don't know what a Pageant is, but I've heard of a Christmas Pudding and a Christmas Cake, so I expect it's something to eat.

DAY 13

I've noticed that, after His manic activity with the camera following the arrival of the Boiled Ham, my dad seems to have lost interest in taking photographs of it. By the time I was its age, I had been photographed much more. This is very good news. When they look back in a few years' time, they'll find an exhaustively detailed and annotated archive of my every nuance of expression, and the records of the Boiled Ham will be just a few snaps.

Tee-hee. The little monster's already learning the downturn of Second Child Syndrome.

DAY 16

I don't like this. The Munchkin is getting far too much of Her attention. While I'm awake, I can usually manage to get Her refocusing on me, but I have no control over what She does while I'm asleep. For all I know, She spends every minute I'm asleep with that little horror in dungarees.

And the trouble is, I do need a lot of sleep these days.

Hmm . . . I must think of something to bring her attention firmly and fully back to me.

DAY 17

When I finally woke up this morning (that's to say, after all the other times I woke up during the night), I knew exactly what to do to make Her my slave. I let Her have the benefit of one of my first smiles.

I did it just as I'd finished my morning feed (well, one of my morning feeds – my Demand Feeding is now so excessive that I'm virtually on a drip). As She drew me away from the nipple, I looked up at Her winsomely, and smiled.

'Oh, has oo got windipops then?' She asked.

Honestly! She is so stupid. Can't She tell the difference between a smile and wind?

I had to do the smile again to make sure She got the point.

The second time, I must say, Her reaction was very gratifying. 'Oh, it's a smile, it's a smile!' She wittered excitely. 'Is oo a big clever smiling Baby?'

And She kept going on about it all through the day. She hardly took any notice of the Munchkin, which was excellent news, so far as I was concerned. Mind you, She did try to get it interested in my smile. 'Look, come and see Baby smile,' She kept saying. 'You give Baby a big smile and Baby'll smile back at you.'

The expression blazed at me from the Munchkin's face could not, by any strength of the imagination, be described as a smile. It was more the look of someone trying to organize a lynch mob.

Knowing it would aggravate the little monster even more, I smiled at it beatifically. Smoke almost came out of its ears! It wouldn't need a mob for the lynching; it'd be quite happy to do the job on its own.

The best bit, though, came this evening, when my awe-struck mum told my dad about my new achievement. 'We had our first smile today,' She cooed. 'And do you know . . . that's more than two weeks earlier than the other one did a first smile.'

Power, power! If I continue to make developmental advances quicker than my older sibling did, its nose is really going to be out of joint!

Huh. I overheard Her saying to Him this evening that the Boiled Ham had done its first smile earlier than I did mine. What they don't seem to realize is that I could have done it whenever I wanted to. I could have done it at two weeks. I could have emerged from the womb grinning all over my face, whistling 'Yankee-Doodle-Dandy' and doing a tap routine!

I just chose not to. I carefully scheduled my first smile for the moment when it would have maximum impact. As I have done with all my other developmental advances.

I don't like the way the wind's blowing, though. Is the timetable of everything the Boiled Ham does going to be compared to mine? Have I now not only got old Smartypants Baby Einstein to contend with? Have I now got competition from within my own home?

Hmm . . . Perhaps I should be thinking seriously about the developmental advances I could be making at the moment . . . ? After all, I don't want to be shamed in two years' time when the Boiled Ham does them quicker.

Maybe this is the moment for me to split my first atom . . . ? Become a Grandmaster at chess . . . ? Broker a peace deal in the Middle East . . . ?

DAY 19

At Playgroup today there was more talk about this Christmas Pageant. Apparently it involves all the children dressing up as characters from some Bible story. Doesn't sound like my sort of thing at all.

DAY 22

Gooey is now about the size of a postage stamp.

I will not be parted from him.

DAY 26

More talk at Playgroup about this Christmas Pageant thing. They've got people for most of the main parts, but they're having difficulty with casting The Ox.

Clearly they went me to play the part.

I don't know. I'll have to think about it.

Thirty-Fifth Month

DAY 3

Today She started the Boiled Ham on solid food. She did it to me at exactly the same time.

The Boiled Ham made a big fuss about the solids, but then it makes a big fuss about everything. Honestly, it is such a baby! So unlike suave, sophisticated me.

But eventually the solids went down. Everything goes down that little monster's ugly throat. It's like having a second Hoover in the house.

The downturn of the Boiled Ham being on solids was that this evening it produced its first post-solids nappy. Wow! Phew! Phwoor! Talk about disgusting!

I think the entire house is going to smell that way forever.

I just hope some Middle-Eastern dictator never gets to hear about it. Otherwise, he's likely to try and kidnap the Boiled Ham to help in the development of his Chemical Weapons Programme.

Actually, on second thoughts, I suppose I could live with the idea of the Boiled Ham stuck permanently in a laboratory somewhere in the desert . . .

DAY 4

Tee-hee. The Boiled Ham had its first experience today of one of the downturns of being on solids – the rigid plastic bib. Immobilized in its high chair with that thing round its neck, the Boiled Ham looked like it was in a pillory.

And what they used to do to people in a pillory was throw rotten food and stuff at them.

I tried a spoonful of mashed potato. It missed and landed on Her – much-neglected – calorie-counting Chart. Pity. I've got the perfect sitting target, but my throwing isn't accurate enough yet to take full advantage of it.

Never mind. I can work on it. Watch out, Boiled Ham. There's a spoonful of mashed potato that's got your name on it.

DAY 7

You just would not believe the way the Boiled Ham gets through nappies! It's an ecological disaster area. I tell you, when the last tree is felled in the last rain forest, there'll be no question where the blame lies. The total destruction of the world as we know it will all have been caused by the Boiled Ham's leaky bum.

DAY 8

One of the great things about being at Playgroup is that if there's any bug going around, you get it. Today there were a lot of kids away. Apparently what's going around this time is a Tummy-Bug.

I started having runny tummy at about ten o'clock in the evening. Got Her up at hourly intervals through the night to deal with it. Needless to say, a complete change of clothes was necessary each time . . .

DAY 9

. . . and then in the morning the Boiled Ham developed the Tummy-Bug too.

We got into quite a good rhythm . . .

9.00 a.m.   She had to change all my clothes.

9.15 a.m.   *She had to change all my clothes.*

9.45 a.m.   She had to change all my clothes.

10.00 a.m.   *She had to change all my clothes.*

10.15 a.m.   She had to change all my clothes.

10.30 a.m.   *She had to change all my clothes . . .*

. . . and so on throughout the day.

This is the first time I've seen any possible advantage in having the Boiled Ham around. When we work together on something like this, two can certainly be more devastating than one.

I'm still a bit suspicious of it, though.

Quite fun, co-operating with the Munchkin today. But I'm not going to make a habit of this kind of thing. I still don't trust the little brute.

DAY 15

They're still on at me at Playgroup to play The Ox in the Christmas Pageant. Apparently you get to wear a headdress with horns on it. There is also a very important line, the highlight of the whole presentation. The Ox has to say, 'Moo.'

Obviously, I'm ideal casting for the part. Miss Heartypants and the others are falling over themselves to try and get me to play it. I don't know, though.

Moo.

DAY 18

Today my mum had a new idea (well, there's a novelty). 'You're growing up so quickly,' She said to me, 'I think we should keep a record of how much bigger you've got.'

OK by me. I am used to all this media attention now. My every move has been chronicled in piles of photograph albums, videos, etc. If She wants to expand the archive, fine. It will obviously be of benefit to the nation when future historians start to write about significant figures of the twenty-first century.

'So, look, here's a nice clean bit of kitchen wall,' She said. 'You stand up against it.'

What on earth is She playing at, I wondered, but to humour the poor old bat I moved to stand facing the bit of wall She'd indicated.

'No, no, the other way round. With your back to the wall.'

I turned round obediently, and then She did something even more peculiar. She got a ruler and put it on top of my head, and then She got a pencil out.

I moved away from the wall to get a better look at what She was doing.

'No, no, you stay there. I can't do it if you move.'

Thinking it's really rather sad that I have a complete nutter for a mum, I moved back into position. She adjusted the ruler on my head . . . and then you'll never guess what She did . . .

She did something totally wicked. She's told me enough times it's totally wicked, so I know just how wicked it is. She scribbled on the wall with Her pencil!!!

'There,' She said. 'I've marked that with the date. And we'll do it again in a month's time, and see how much you've grown!' Then She went on, 'Pity we can't do the same for the New Baby, but we can't get the New Baby to stand up straight against the wall, can we?'

I don't know. I can think of a few ways of stringing the little monster up.

35 months—

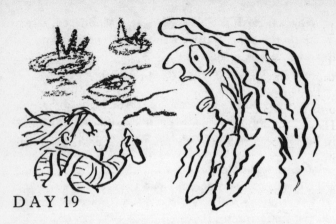

DAY 19

Life is so unfair! Parents are just so unreasonable!

Left to my own devices in the kitchen this morning, I thought I would give Her a nice surprise by showing Her how well my artistic skills are developing. After what She'd done yesterday, I knew that the ban on scribbling on the kitchen wall had been lifted, so I got out my crayons and covered all the area I could reach with a beautiful, brightly coloured impressionist display of water lilies, roses, lakes and rivers, rather in the style of Monet.

But did I get any gratitude? Did I hell?

Rather than congratulating me and immediately whisking off the relevant piece of wall to the National Gallery, She bawled me out like nobody's business.

She even had the nerve to give me a smack! A smack! Now I'm back in post-Boiled-Ham-traumatic-stress nappies during the day, the smack itself didn't hurt too much, but that's not the point. It's the principle that counts here.

It's an infringement of my Civil Liberties. I'm going to take her all the way up to the European Court of Human Rights for this.

DAY 20

That marking up on the wall business has made me think about growing, and it's got me a bit worried.

I'm growing OK, but in the past few months it's only probably been an inch or two. Whereas the Boiled Ham . . . in the three months or so since She found it in the hospital and brought it home, it's nearly doubled in size.

If it doubles in size every three months, it'll soon be bigger than me. And not long after that, it'll be so big it won't fit in the house.

No wonder I'm worried.

DAY 22

I've finally given in and agreed to play The Ox in the Christmas Pageant. The relief on Miss Heartypants' face when I said 'Yes' was pathetic to behold.

DAY 24   [1 2 3 4 5 6 7 8 9 10]

At Playgroup this morning, Miss Heartypants and the other Helpers were on about counting again. They're really obsessed with it. There are friezes of numbers all around the walls, and lots of the toys are covered with numbers. Clearly, the Playgroup Helpers are dead worried about us going into the outside world without being able to count.

I can't really see why they worry. The grown-ups I know don't seem to have mastered the basic skill of counting and yet they get through life all right. For instance, my mum can't count. The number of times I've heard Her say to Him when He wants Her to go up to bed, 'I'll just be five minutes.' And then She falls asleep in front of the television, and it's a lot more than five minutes.

My dad's no better. If He's in the pub – or even at home – and someone says to Him 'Get you another drink?' He always replies, 'Oh, all right then, just the one.'

And it never is! He can't count for toffee. When He says 'Just the one' He means at least three.

So, if it doesn't matter for grown-ups, I don't see why we should be bothered about it at our age.

And the Playgroup Helpers don't have to worry about me, anyway. I can count already. You'd be able to too, if your hands and feet had suffered as many counting games as mine have.

Virtually every night since I was born, my toes have had to go through the bedtime ritual of the old 'This little piggy went to market' routine. It's most peculiar. I've never really understood it. I mean, I understand the words, but what are they saying in a cosmic sense?

What, I ask myself, is going to happen to the individual toes in later life? Are we meant to assume that the one who 'stayed at home' suffered from agoraphobia? Will the one who 'had roast beef' contract BSE and drop off? Are we meant to assume that the one who 'had none' is vegetarian?

The only bit that ever made any sense to me was the one who 'went wee-wee-wee all the way home'. Every night when we got to that bit, I happily followed suit.

Anyway, as I say, all that indoctrination means that I can count. I do it better on my hands. It's dead easy. You just go along the fingers. 'One – Two – Three – Four . . .'

Then comes the tricky bit. You have to remember that the last one isn't a finger. No, it's a fum.

So you go, 'One – Two – Three – Four – Fum.' Easy-peasy. I can count up to fum.

DAY 29

We did a counting rhyme at Playgroup today. And Miss Heartypants, who was leading us, got it wrong.

She tried to get us all singing,

One – Two – Three – Four – Five –
Once I caught a fish alive.

Clearly that's nonsense. Don't know where she got that 'Five' from. It should be 'One – Two – Three – Four – Fum'.

I tried to work out why she should deliberately try to mislead us. Then I realized. It's censorship. They won't let us do the real version of the song, because they don't think it's right for nicely brought up little things like us.

It didn't take long to work out how the song should have gone. The clue's in the rhyme. The original version must have been:

One – Two – Three – Four – Fum –
Once I caught a fish's bum.

But they wouldn't want us going around saying that.

Thirty-Sixth Month

DAY 4

The Helpers seem to have given up all other Playgroup activities in favour of rehearsals for the Christmas Pageant. It's quite touching to see how excited some of the little ones are getting about it.

The girl playing Mary, for instance. She's a right little madam, and it's entirely gone to her head. She thinks what we're doing is a play about a girl called Mary who had a baby. Rather sweet, really. Because, of course, everyone knows that in fact it's a play about The Ox.

I practised my 'Moo' today. They were all very impressed. Real talent will always shine through.

DAY 8

Hysteria today at the Christmas Pageant rehearsal. I got my cue to say, 'Moo!', but instead of saying it, I let my bottom do the talking! A really huge one.

How everyone roared!

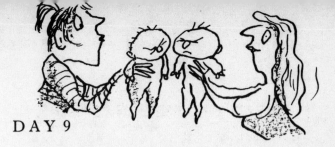

DAY 9

A friend of Hers, who'd also got a New Baby, came round for coffee this morning. They were very competitive, the two mums together, each trying to prove that their baby was prettier, or cleverer, or more developed than the other one.

In my view, both babies were revolting, but, if you did have to make comparisons, well, there was no contest. I'd always thought the Boiled Ham was the ugliest, most inept, slow-witted baby in the world, but, compared to this new one, it's a genius, with the ability to write *War and Peace* and play Elgar's Cello Concerto while running a World Record Hundred Metres.

I actually got quite cross when this other mother was saying disparaging things about the Boiled Ham. Much as it repels me to admit the fact, the Boiled Ham is my flesh and blood. And if outsiders want to start attacking it, well, they'll have to take me on first.

Not that I like the Boiled Ham or anything. I don't want you to get the wrong impression. I'm not getting sentimental in my old age. It's just that blood is thicker than water, that's all.

DAY 10

Oh dear. She got out Her old exercise bicycle today. She managed about ten minutes before running out of puff and collapsing.

It's pathetic. She's trying to get Her figure back after the second baby.

Fat chance, sweetheart. She never got it back after me.

No, She'll just have to come to terms with the fact. The incalculable enrichment that having me has brought into Her life has not been without its costs.

For a start, She'll never see a waist again. Or a Size 10.

But, apart from the daily blessing of my presence, there are a few other things my arrival has brought Her. Stretch marks and varicose veins! Tee-hee!

She got an exercise bicycle out today, and had ten minutes on it.

It's pathetic. She's trying to get Her figure back after having me.

Fat chance, sweetheart.

As I was watching Her pathetic efforts with considerable amusement, I looked across at the Munchkin, and saw that it was smiling.

The Boiled Ham seemed quite amused by our mum's antics. Perhaps the little beast has a sense of humour.

If we find the same things funny, is it possible that one day we might become friends?

If we find the same things funny, is it possible that one day we might become friends?

No way.

Forget it. Anyone would find the sight of our mum on an exercise bike funny.

DAY 11

I'm getting a bit cross about Her fooling around on Her exercise bicycle when She should be concentrating on making my costume for the Christmas Pageant. Two of the Wise Men, and the Ass, and the Young Madam who's playing Mary, and Buddha, and Krishna and Muhammad (I'm not quite sure what those three are doing there, but ours is a very politically correct Playgroup) have all got their costumes already. Right prats they look, too.

But at least their mums have made an effort. Whenever I mention it to mine, She says, 'Yes, I will do it. I will do it. I'm just so busy with the Baby these days.'

Huh. She should get Her priorities sorted. She shouldn't be concentrating on the Boiled Ham when She's got real theatrical talent in Her family. My performance as The Ox will be talked about for decades to come, I know it, and She'll be able to spend Her declining years bathed in reflected glory. The least She can do now is to get my costume sorted.

DAY 12

She showed me my so-called The Ox costume today. What a let-down!

I mean, what I had in mind was something rather magnificent . . . you know, the fine head of a noble beast with rampant horns rising proudly into the sky – a sort of cross between the Minotaur and the *Monarch of the Glen*.

But what She came up with was a kind of floppy brown felt hat. The ears were floppy. Even the horns were floppy. They dangled down either side, making me look like an apologetic spaniel.

DAY 13

We had a rehearsal for the Christmas Pageant today, with us all dressed in our costumes. I was really humiliated. A new mum who was coming to look round the Playgroup saw me in my The Ox gear and said, 'Oh, I didn't know there was a Gerbil in the Nativity story.'

DAY 16

A scene at Playgroup today from the Young Madam who's playing Mary. She made a big fuss because she said the doll they'd given her to be Baby Jesus didn't look anything like a real baby. Huh, a bad actress always blames her props, and she is a truly dreadful actress. Apart from anything else, she keeps dropping the doll all the time.

One of the Helpers said, 'Well, maybe we should try to find a real baby to be in the Pageant.'

I very nearly suggested the Boiled Ham. I wouldn't mind if the Young Madam who's playing Mary kept dropping that all the time.

DAY 17

We had a 'run-through' today. All of it. The way the presentation works is: Miss Heartypants reads bits of a story about some baby being born in a stable (that sounds like a job for the Social Workers, if ever I heard one). And then at key points, some of us kids have to do something.

Only some of us, though. Some can't be trusted with doing anything. Buddha, Krishna and Muhammad just stand around all the time looking like they can't think why they're there (which, given the circumstances, is perhaps not such a surprise).

And some can't be trusted to say words. I mean, the Young Madam who's playing Mary's not allowed to say anything. The Helpers know she'd cock it up. No, all she's allowed to do is, when Miss Heartypants says, 'And Mary put the baby in the manger,' place the doll in this Sainsbury's mushroom box. (They've said they're going to put something round it, but nothing's happened yet – it's still covered with pictures of mushrooms.)

And the Young Madam who's playing Mary even manages to cock that up. Nine times out of ten, in rehearsal, she drops the doll so that it misses the Sainsbury's mushroom box completely.

Then a very few of us are allowed actual words. The Wise Men say what presents they have brought for the doll. Miss Heartypants cues them in.

She reads, 'One of the Wise Men brought . . .' and the first kid says, 'Gold'.

She reads, 'Another of the Wise Men brought . . .' and the second kid says, 'Frankincense'. (You might think that's a difficult word for someone of our age to say, but when I tell you that the Second Wise Man is being played by Baby Einstein . . . say no more, huh?)

Then Miss Heartypants reads, 'And the Third Wise Man brought . . .' and the third kid is meant to say, 'Myrrh'.

But, honestly, with that kid it's a lottery. He might say anything. 'Biccit.' 'Blobby.' 'Cheese.' 'Grommet.' 'Willy.' 'Spiderman.' You just never know. Every rehearsal is a new excitement.

Only two other members of the cast are allowed to speak. The Ox and The Ass. I'm still a bit worried about the order. Obviously, it's right that The Ox comes first, but that means I speak first. So the one who has the last word, whose voice remains ringing in the audience's ears as they go out, is The Ass.

And in this production, The Ass is, I'm afraid, not the greatest actor ever to hit the stage. For a start, it's a girl, and surely an ass should be male, shouldn't it?

And then she says 'Baa'. Asses shouldn't say 'Baa'. They should bray, shouldn't they? But this little prat can't bray. All she can do is say 'Baa'. And the Helpers – with a lack of professionalism which I find distressing in any production that I'm involved in – have just accepted that.

My only comfort is that, in the minds of the audience, her pathetic little 'Baa' will be lost in the lingering memory of my robust and moving 'Moo!'

The way the lines go, incidentally, is that Miss Heartypants reads, 'And even the farm animals wanted to say hello to the Baby Jesus. The Ox said . . .' And

then I say, 'Moo'. '. . . and the Ass said . . .' And then the Ass says, 'Baa'.

The run-through today was a complete – but complete – shambles. Still, you know what they say about a bad Dress Rehearsal . . .

DAY 18

Today we did the Christmas Pageant. The first sign that anything was different from an ordinary morning was that the mums stayed around after they'd delivered us at the Playgroup. (Normally, they can't wait to get out of the door.) There was even the odd dad there too (and I use the word 'odd' advisedly).

Even worse, my mum had brought the Boiled Ham with Her. It was asleep, and She had it strapped on Her front in one of those sling jobs. I felt dead ashamed. The other mums had much prettier accessories.

All the parents hung around one side of the room, laughing and sniggering, while we were all on the other side of the room, getting changed into our costumes. I didn't like this. I thought it was a bit public.

And it took away the surprise element. I wanted to make an entrance when I came in as The Ox (even if I did look like The Gerbil).

Finally everyone was more or less in costume, and the Christmas Pageant could begin. Even before it did, though, the flashlights were going and the camcorders were whirring. Each parent seemed to want to capture for posterity every movement of their ugly little brat – even if it was only a shepherd with a tea towel pinned round its head.

I was a bit ambivalent about the photography and video aspect. Part of me wanted to have my memorable performance as The Ox immortalized, but another part wasn't too keen on me being immortalized as a Gerbil.

In fact, the decision was taken out of my hands, because my mum had forgotten to bring either the camera or the camcorder. Honestly! She has got so absent-minded since that bloody Boiled Ham's been around.

The first thing the Young Madam who's playing Mary did – even before she'd really made her entrance properly – was to drop the baby. The assembled mums and dads thought this was hilarious. Oh no, I thought, *that* kind of audience. Just here for the cheap laughs.

Never mind, though. I knew they had at least one moment of real drama ahead. Just wait till they got to my 'Moo'. I'd chill their blood with that. I'd make sure that wiped the smiles off their faces.

When the Young Madam who's playing Mary was meant to show the Baby Jesus to the Wise Men, she managed to drop it again. That too got a huge laugh from the audience.

And they had another, predictably enough, when they got to the Wise Men's presents.

'One of the Wise Men brought . . .' read Miss Heartypants, and the first kid says, 'Gold'. Spot on.

Miss Heartypants continued, 'Another of the Wise Men brought . . .' and the second kid says, 'Frankincense'. Absolutely perfectly. (The audience's muted

reaction to Baby Einstein's achievement once again bore out the old saying that 'Nobody likes a Smartarse'.)

Then we all waited with bated breath, as Miss Heartypants read, 'And the Third Wise Man brought . . .'

There was a long pause, while the Third Wise Man made up his mind. Then, loudly, he said, 'Poo!'

We all laughed at that, kids and parents. Well, you have to admit, it was quite witty.

No more laughs, though, as my big moment approached. This was good. I wanted them in sober mood, so that they'd be more receptive to the subtleties of my 'Moo'.

The climax of the play grew ever closer. Miss Heartypants read, 'And even the farm animals wanted to say hello to the Baby Jesus. The Ox said . . .'

I thought I'd give it a pause, a long one for full dramatic impact. Then I took a big breath and—

Just as I was about to speak, there was a wail from the auditorium. Not so much a wail, actually, as a shriek.

The audience all roared with laughter. My 'Moo' was entirely lost in the noise.

The bloody Boiled Ham had chosen that exact moment to wake up!

Huh. In later life it's going to pay for that blatant piece of upstaging!

Tee-hee! I really screwed up the Munchkin's big moment today! It's got to learn – no one tries to take the limelight away from me and survives!

DAY 19

My last morning at Playgroup. With huge relief, I heard my mum saying to Miss Heartypants, 'I don't think we'll be doing two mornings a week at Playgroup next term.'

Hooray, hooray, I thought. Finally She has realized how restricting all this regimentation is to a fine young mind like mine.

And then She dashed my hopes by saying, 'I think we should step it up to five mornings a week.'

What? And when am I ever going to get any time to myself?

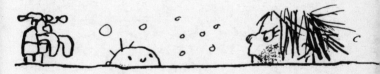

DAY 20

Up until now She's always bathed the Boiled Ham in a baby bath, but tonight She put in it the big bath with me. I was pretty affronted at first. This was my space!

She had the nerve tonight to put me in the same bath as the Munchkin! I was furious. I don't want to mix with specimens like that!

The only good thing about Her bathing the Boiled Ham at the same time as me is that She has to lean right over the bath to hold it. This puts Her in perfect splashing range – and She can't move away because She daren't let go of the Boiled Ham!

The only good thing about being in this big bath, compared to the baby bath, is the amount of water in it. If I kick like mad, it goes all over Her.

When the Boiled Ham and I splashed together, it was like She'd been hit by a tidal wave.

When the Munchkin and I got a proper rhythm going, it was like She'd been hit by a tidal wave.

This opens up a whole new set of possibilities for bathtime mayhem. Tee-hee.

I think, from now on, bathtime's going to be FUN. Tee-hee.

DAY 25

We went through the whole Christmas routine again today. The Boiled Ham seemed more interested in the wrapping paper than it was in the presents. Is it stupid or what?

And I still didn't get my £249.99 Super-Mega-CD-Blaster. It's awful growing up as a deprived child.

Christmas today. I was given piles of presents. They seemed to find it funny when I played with the wrapping paper rather than the presents. Oh well, if it turns them on . . .

DAY 29

A terrible disaster today!

I dropped Gooey, who is now the size of a bit of belly button fluff, on the floor just as She was doing the cleaning, and She hoovered him up!

I wailed and wailed, shouting 'Gooey!' and pointing at the Hoover bag. Eventually, She understood, and emptied the entire contents on to a sheet of newspaper. I made Her go through every bit of fluff inside until She found Gooey.

She passed him across to me.

I don't think I can go through that kind of experience of loss again. I need to keep Gooey somewhere safe.

So, after my Mother had gone out of the room, I thought of a way that Gooey and I can be together for ever.

I swallowed him.

DAY 31

Coo. Just look at the way I've come on in the last four months. I'm good-looking, mature, intelligent, with any number of highly sophisticated skills at my command.

The only cloud in the sunny skies of my existence has been the Munchkin. Mind you, I'm learning to live with that. It's an unprepossessing little horror, but on the other hand, there are moments when, working together, we can cause even more mayhem for our parents than either one of us could on our own.

I'm not suggesting our partnership is equal. Good heavens, no. There's no question about the balance of power in this family, you see. My Parents are my devoted slaves and . . . I'M THE ONE IN CHARGE.

Well, I'm nearly three now – good-looking, mature, intelligent, and with any number of highly sophisticated skills at my command.

The only downturn of this year has been the arrival of the Boiled Ham. It's still here, so I've reluctantly come to the conclusion that they really are intending to keep it. But then they never did have any taste.

On the other hand, there are moments when even the Boiled Ham can be quite useful. It's sometimes handy to have a helper in the business of making one's parents' life hell.

But the arrival of the Boiled Ham hasn't changed the basic balance of power in this family. Oh no, in spite of all the changes in this household during the last year, my parents remain my devoted slaves and . . . I'M STILL THE ONE IN CHARGE.